TED WILLIAMS

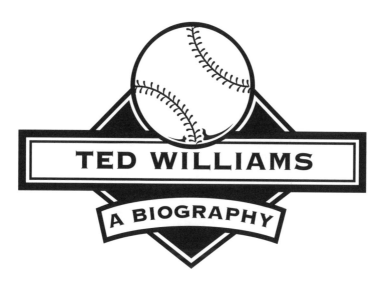

TED WILLIAMS
A BIOGRAPHY

BRUCE MARKUSEN

BASEBALL'S ALL-TIME GREATEST HITTERS

GREENWOOD PRESS
WESTPORT, CONNECTICUT • LONDON

Library of Congress Cataloging-in-Publication Data

Markusen, Bruce.
    Ted Williams, a biography / Bruce Markusen.
       p. cm.—(Baseball's all-time greatest hitters)
    Includes bibliographical references (p.   ) and index.
    ISBN 0–313–32867–6 (alk. paper)
       1. Williams, Ted, 1918– 2. Baseball players—United States—Biography.
  I. Title: Ted Williams. II. Title. III. Series.
GV865.W5M27   2004
796.357'092—dc22   2004047536
[B]

British Library Cataloguing in Publication Data is available.

Library of Congress Catalog Card Number: 2004047536
ISBN: 0–313–32867–6

First published in 2004

Greenwood Press, 88 Post Road West, Westport, CT 06881
An imprint of Greenwood Publishing Group, Inc.
www.greenwood.com

Printed in the United States of America

The paper used in this book complies with the
Permanent Paper Standard issued by the National
Information Standards Organization (Z39.48–1984).

10 9 8 7 6 5 4 3 2 1

Every reasonable effort has been made to trace the owners of copyright materials in this book,
but in some instances this has proven impossible. The author and publisher will be glad to receive information leading to more complete acknowledgments in subsequent printings of the
book and in the meantime extend their apologies for any omissions.

This biography of Ted Williams is dedicated to my wife, Sue Markusen. She has changed my life and made it so much better.

CONTENTS

Contents

SERIES FOREWORD

The volumes in Greenwood's "Baseball's All-Time Greatest Hitters" series present the life stories of the players who, through their abilities to hit for average, for power, or for both, most helped their teams at the plate. Much thought was given to the players selected for inclusion in this series. In some cases, the selection of certain players was a given. **Ty Cobb, Rogers Hornsby**, and **Joe Jackson** hold the three highest career averages in baseball history: .367, .358, and .356, respectively. **Babe Ruth**, who single-handedly brought the sport out of its "Dead Ball" era and transformed baseball into a home-run hitters game, hit 714 home runs (a record that stood until 1974) while also hitting .342 over his career. **Lou Gehrig**, now known primarily as the man whose consecutive-games record Cal Ripken Jr. broke in 1995, hit .340 and knocked in more than 100 runs eleven seasons in a row, totaling 1,995 before his career was cut short by ALS. **Ted Williams**, the last man in either league to hit .400 or better in a season (.406 in 1941), is widely regarded as possibly the best hitter ever, a man whose fanatical dedication raised hitting to the level of both science and art.

Two players set career records that, for many, define the art of hitting. **Hank Aaron** set career records for home runs (755) and RBIs (2,297). He also maintained a .305 career average over twenty-three seasons, a remarkable feat for someone primarily known as a home-run hitter. **Pete Rose** had ten seasons with 200 or more hits and won three batting titles on his way to establishing his famous record of 4,256 career hits. Some critics have claimed that both players' records rest more on longevity than excellence. To that I would say there is something to be said about longevity and, in both cases, the player's excellence was the reason why he had the opportunity to keep playing, to keep tallying hits for his team. A base hit is the mark of a successful plate appearance; a home run is the apex of an at-bat. Accordingly, we could hardly have a series titled "Baseball's All-Time Greatest Hitters" without including the two men who set the career records in these categories.

Joe DiMaggio holds another famous mark: fifty-six consecutive games in which he obtained a base hit. Many have called this baseball's most unbreakable record. (The player who most closely approached that mark was Pete Rose, who hit safely in forty-four consecutive games in 1978.) In his thirteen seasons, DiMaggio hit .325 with 361 home runs and 1,537 RBIs. This means he *averaged* 28 home runs and 118 RBIs per season. MVPs have been awarded to sluggers in various years with lesser stats than what DiMaggio achieved in an "average" season.

Because **Stan Musial** played his entire career with the Cardinals in St. Louis—once considered the western frontier of the baseball world in the days before baseball came to California—he did not receive the press of a DiMaggio. But Musial compiled a career average of .331, with 3,630 hits (ranking fourth all time) and 1,951 RBIs (fifth all time). His hitting prowess was so respected around the league that Brooklyn Dodgers fans once dubbed him "The Man," a nickname he still carries today.

Willie Mays was a player who made his fame in New York City and then helped usher baseball into the modern era when he moved with the Giants to San Francisco. Mays did everything well and with flair. His over-the-shoulder catch in the 1954 World Series was perhaps his most famous moment, but his hitting was how Mays most tormented his opponents. Over twenty-two seasons the "Say Hey" kid hit .302 and belted 660 home runs.

Only four players have reached the 600-home-run milestone: Mays, Aaron, Ruth, and **Barry Bonds**, who achieved that feat in 2002. Bonds, the only active player included in this series, broke the single-season home-run record when he smashed 73 for the San Francisco Giants in 2001. In the 2002 National League Championship Series, St. Louis Cardinals pitchers were so leery of pitching to him that they walked him ten times in twenty-one plate appearances. In the World Series, the Anaheim Angels walked him thirteen times in thirty appearances. He finished the Series with a .471 batting average, an on-base percentage of .700, and a slugging percentage of 1.294.

As with most rankings, this series omits some great names. Jimmie Foxx, Tris Speaker, and Tony Gwynn would have battled for a hypothetical thirteenth volume. And it should be noted that this series focuses on players and their performance within Major League Baseball; otherwise, sluggers such as Josh Gibson from the Negro Leagues and Japan's Sadaharu Oh would have merited consideration.

There are names such as Cap Anson, Ed Delahanty, and Billy Hamilton who appear high up on the list of career batting average. However, a number of these players played during the late 1800s, when the rules of baseball were drastically different. For example, pitchers were not allowed to throw overhand until 1883, and foul balls weren't counted as strikes until 1901 (1903 in the American League). Such players as Anson and company undeniably were the stars of their day, but baseball has evolved greatly since then, into a game in which hitters must now cope with night games, relief pitchers, and split-fingered fastballs.

Ultimately, a list of the "greatest" anything is somewhat subjective, but Greenwood offers these players as twelve of the finest examples of hitters throughout history. Each volume focuses primarily on the playing career of the subject: his early years in school, his years in semi-pro and/or minor league baseball, his entrance into the majors, and his ascension to the status of a legendary hitter. But even with the greatest of players, baseball is only part of the story, so the player's life before and after baseball is given significant consideration. And because no one can exist in a vacuum, the authors often take care to recreate the cultural and historical contexts of the time—an approach that is especially relevant to the multidisciplinary ways in which sports are studied today.

Batter up.

ROB KIRKPATRICK
GREENWOOD PUBLISHING
FALL 2003

ACKNOWLEDGMENTS

A number of people have been generous with their time and talents in helping put together this book. I owe special thanks to Bill Nowlin, one of the leading experts on the career and life of Ted Williams. Bill graciously agreed to read the manuscript, making a number of corrections and helpful suggestions. His insight on Williams has been critical in compiling accurate information about Ted's life. I'd also like to thank Sue Markusen for careful proofreading assistance and Amanda Pinney for diligent fact-checking of the entire manuscript. Finally, special thanks to David Pietrusza, the co-author of the terrific book, *Teddy Ballgame: My Life in Pictures*, for answering questions and offering anecdotes about Williams during a visit to the Hall of Fame.

CHRONOLOGY

1918   Future Hall-of-Famer Ted Williams is born in San Diego, California, on August 30.

1936   Seventeen-year-old Williams signs a contract for $150 a month with the San Diego Padres of the Pacific Coast League (PCL). In making his professional debut, Williams hits an uncharacteristic .271 with no home runs and 11 RBIs in 107 regular season at-bats.

1937   Williams hits .291 with 23 home runs and 98 RBIs in his first full season as a starting outfielder with the Padres. After the 1937 season, Boston Red Sox general manager Eddie Collins purchases the 19-year-old Williams for two players and $25,000 cash.

1938   Williams attends his first major league spring training, joining the Red Sox in Sarasota, Florida. Assigned to Boston's minor league affiliate in Minneapolis, Williams hits .366 with 43 home runs and 142 RBIs, winning the American Association (AA) Triple Crown.

1939   Williams makes the Boston Red Sox Opening Day roster. On April 20, the 20-year-old Williams makes his major league debut in the Red Sox 2–0 loss to the New York Yankees. Williams strikes out twice, but also blasts a 407-foot double to right center field. On April 23, Williams hits his first major league home run. The outfielder finishes his first major league season with a .327 batting average, 31 home runs, and a rookie record of 145 RBIs.

1940   The Red Sox put up a bullpen in front of the right-field fence, thereby short-ening the dimensions of the right-field wall. The area will soon be referred to as "Williamsburg." The Sox move Williams to left field so that he will not have to deal with the sun field, which is right field, at Fenway Park. During the 1940 season, Williams bats .344, a seventeen-point improvement over his rookie season, but his power numbers dip from his first season.

1941   In the spring, Williams chips his ankle bone, delaying his ability to start the season in left field. On May 15, Williams starts a twenty-three-game hitting streak. He bats .487 during the stretch. Williams enters the 1941 All-Star break with a .405 average, 16 home runs, and 62 RBIs.

On July 8, Williams hits a dramatic 2-out, 3-run homer in the bottom of the ninth inning, giving the American League a 7–5 win in the All Star Game. Williams' clout, coming in Detroit, overshadows a two-homer game by National League star Arky Vaughan.

On September 28, Williams goes 6 for 8 in a season-ending doubleheader to raise his final average to .406. Williams, who could have sat out the game and "protected" a .400 average, becomes the last major leaguer to reach the mile-stone, and the first since Bill Terry of the New York Giants in 1930. However, despite reaching the .400 mark, Williams does not win the American League's MVP Award. Instead, the award goes to Joe DiMaggio, who compiled a fifty-six-game hitting streak in 1941.

On December 7, the attack on Pearl Harbor occurs, spurring U.S. entry into World War II. The tragedy at Pearl Harbor has a huge impact on Williams, who will be called into service.

1942   In May, Williams enlists in the Navy air corps. After finishing out the 1942 season with the Red Sox, Williams reports for military duty. He will miss more than three seasons of major league play while serving in World War II.

1946   On January 12, Williams receives his discharge from the U.S. Marine Air Corps after a three-year stint serving in World War II. In spite of his long absence from competitive baseball, Williams returns to the major leagues in 1946 by hitting .342, with 38 home runs and 123 RBIs.

On July 9, in the All Star Game, Williams homers on the famed blooper pitch thrown by Rip Sewell of the Pittsburgh Pirates. Williams finishes the game with 2 home runs, 2 singles, and a record-setting 5 RBIs in the American League's 12–0 win.

On July 14, Lou Boudreau of the Cleveland Indians collects four doubles and a home run in the first game of a doubleheader against the Red Sox. How-ever, Williams overshadows Boudreau by hitting three homers and driving in eight runs to lead the Sox to an 11–10 win. In the second game of the double-header, Boudreau uses an unusual shift against Williams, but only in situations with no one on base. He places six defenders to the right of second base and leaves only one to the left of second base, with the catcher and pitcher forced to remain in their normal positions. This alignment becomes known as the "Williams Shift" or the "Boudreau Shift."

On September 13, Williams defies the "Boudreau Shift" by hitting an inside-the-park home run to left field (the only inside-the-park home run of his career). The opposite field homer gives Boston a 1–0 victory and clinches the American League pennant for the Red Sox.

In the 1946 World Series, St. Louis Cardinals manager Eddie Dyer also decides to employ the shift. At one point, Williams tries to bunt against the shift. He reaches on a hit but otherwise struggles against Cardinals pitching. With Williams a nonfactor at the plate, the Red Sox lose the World Series in seven games.

On November 15, Williams wins his first Most Valuable Player Award. Williams had won the Triple Crown in 1941, but lost the MVP race to Joe DiMaggio of the New York Yankees. This time, Williams defeats Detroit Tigers ace Hal Newhouser, a two-time winner of the award who places second in the balloting.

1947 Williams wins his second Triple Crown, but the Red Sox fall to third place in the American League. On November 27, Joe DiMaggio edges Williams to capture his third American League MVP Award. DiMaggio wins the award even though Williams leads the league in batting average, home runs, and RBIs. Williams receives only three first-place votes.

1948 The Sox win three straight games toward the end of the season to tie the Cleveland Indians for first place in the standings. In those three games, Williams plays a significant role, with 2-for-2, 2-for-2, and 2-for-4 efforts at the plate.

1949 On October 2, the New York Yankees win the American League pennant by defeating the Red Sox, 5–3. Jerry Coleman's 3-run double provides the winning margin, while Williams falls short of both the American League batting title and the Triple Crown.

1950 On June 8, the Red Sox establish a major league record for the most runs in one game as they rip the St. Louis Browns, 29–4, at Fenway Park. Bobby Doerr hits 3 home runs and drives in eight, while Williams and Walt Dropo each slam 2 home runs. On July 13, Williams undergoes an operation to remove several bone fragments from his elbow; he broke the elbow crashing into the fence trying to track down a drive by Ralph Kiner. Williams eventually returns from the injury and hits .350 over the second half to finish the season with a .317 average.

1952 In January, the U.S. Marines announce that they will recall Williams into active duty to serve in the Korean War. On April 30, Williams plays his final game before leaving for military duty in Korea. In his last at-bat on "Ted

Williams Day" at Fenway Park, the "Splendid Splinter" blasts a game-winning, 2-run home run against Dizzy Trout of the Detroit Tigers. The home run gives the Red Sox a 5–3 win; many fans assume it will be the final game for the 33-year-old Williams.

1953 On February 16, Williams crash-lands his fighter plane after flying a combat mission during the Korean War. Williams survives the landing and returns to the Red Sox during the 1953 season. During his term in Korea, Williams flies thirty-nine missions. On August 6, Williams makes his first appearance with the Red Sox after his military stint in Korea. Williams, who pops out in a pinch-hit appearance, finishes the season with a .407 batting average.

1954 On March 1, Williams fractures his collarbone on the first day of spring training. The injury occurs as Williams dives for a ball hit by teammate Hoot Evers. As a result, Williams misses Opening Day and the first thirty-six games of the regular season. On May 16, Williams returns to the Red Sox lineup and goes 8 for 9 with 2 home runs, a double, and 7 RBIs in a doubleheader. However, Williams' offensive heroics do not prevent the Red Sox from losing both games to the Detroit Tigers.

1957 On June 13, the 39-year-old Williams hits three home runs in the Red Sox 9–2 win over the Cleveland Indians. Williams, who had a 3-homer game earlier in the year, becomes the first American Leaguer to hit 3 home runs in a game twice in the same season. On November 22, Mickey Mantle barely edges Williams in the American League's MVP voting. Mantle gains 233 votes to Williams' 209 votes. Mantle batted .365 with 34 home runs for the first-place New York Yankees, while the 39-year-old Williams batted .388 with 38 home runs for the third-place Red Sox.

1958 On February 6, Ted Williams signs a one-year contract with the Red Sox. The contract is reported to be worth between $135,000 to $150,000. In either case, Williams becomes the highest-paid player in the history of the franchise. During the 1958 season, Williams claims his sixth—and last—batting title. He bats .328 for the season, finishing just ahead of teammate Pete Runnels, who led the race during the stretch run.

1959 The Red Sox became the final major league team to integrate when they promote infielder Elijah "Pumpsie" Green from the minor leagues. Williams is one of the few Red Sox who makes an effort to treat Green well, warming up with him prior to games.

1960 On June 17, Ted Williams becomes the fourth major league player to hit his 500th home run, joining Babe Ruth, Jimmie Foxx, and Mel Ott. Williams' 2-

run shot at Municipal Stadium against Wynn Hawkins helps the Red Sox to a 3–1 win over the Cleveland Indians. Williams reaches other milestones in 1960, including 2,000 walks and 1,800 RBIs.

On August 17, the *Sporting News* names Williams "Player of the Decade" for the 1950s. From 1950 to 1959, the "Splendid Splinter" won two batting titles, led the American League in slugging percentage twice, and also led the league in walks twice.

On September 28, Ted Williams plays in his final game. Prior to the game, the Red Sox hold a simple ceremony and retire Williams' uniform No. 9. In his final at-bat, Williams faces Jack Fisher and smashes a home run. Williams powers the ball 450 feet into the right-field bleachers at Fenway Park. Williams' 521st home run places him third on the all-time list, behind only Babe Ruth and Jimmie Foxx, both former Red Sox.

1966   On July 25, Williams and Casey Stengel are inducted into the Hall of Fame in Cooperstown, New York. Both men make memorable speeches. Williams calls for the election of former Negro Leagues stars to the Hall of Fame. Five years later, Satchel Paige becomes the first Negro League standout to take his place in Cooperstown.

1969   On January 18, the last-place Washington Senators announce that Ted Williams has been named their new manager.

On February 21, Williams returns to baseball by officially signing a five-year contract to manage the Senators.

On April 7, Williams makes his managerial debut for the Senators. Williams loses his first game to the New York Yankees, 8–4, on Opening Day at RFK Stadium. A crowd of over 45,000 fans, including President Richard Nixon, packs the stadium. Under Williams' leadership, the Senators finish the season with a record of 86–76, the best mark in the franchise's history. Williams manages the Senators for three seasons before moving with the team to Texas in 1972.

1972   Williams steps down as skipper of the Texas Rangers at the end of the 1972 season, never to return to managing.

1999   On July 13, just prior to the All Star Game at Fenway Park, an 80-year-old Williams rides around the ballpark's warning track in a golf cart before making a memorable stop near the mound, where he is joined by many of the game's current stars.

2002   On July 5, Ted Williams dies after a lengthy illness, which included a series of debilitating strokes. He was 83 years old. On July 22, the Red Sox hold a moving ceremony at Fenway Park, dubbed "A Celebration of An American Hero," in memory of Williams.

Ted Williams produces baseball's most classic swing. *National Baseball Hall of Fame Library, Cooperstown, N.Y.*

INTRODUCTION

Ted Williams was known, in particular, for two memorable quotations about the game of baseball and the art of hitting. He often said, with the exact phrasing sometimes changing from interview to interview, that "hitting was the toughest thing to do in all of sports." While some followers of other sports might make an argument for skills pertinent to their pastimes, Williams found agreement from more than a few athletes, sportswriters, and broadcasters. In a more sentimental mood, a philosophical Williams made reference to the personal dream that he had maintained ever since his youth. "All I want out of life is that when I walk down the street folks will say, 'There goes the greatest hitter who ever lived.'" Once again, Williams' statement of aspiration might have found some objection from supporters of the likes of Babe Ruth and Barry Bonds, but more than a few fans have developed the strong belief that Williams had indeed fulfilled his wish. If so, we might be tempted to combine both of Williams' famous quotations and conclude that he became the greatest and most accomplished achiever of the most difficult task in all of professional sport.

While such a proclamation is debatable, the following statement is probably not: *No one approached the act of hitting with more passion than Ted Williams.* He practiced hitting to the point of exhaustion; he loved hitting to the point of obsession. From his boyhood days to his retirement years, no one dedicated as much time to the improvement and refinement of swinging a bat, of hitting a pitched ball. And it was not a skill that he kept to himself. As a coach and manager in his later years, he did his best to teach younger men the keys and secrets to becoming successful as a hitter. He wanted others to share the satisfying experience of hitting a baseball with the kind of excellence that he had done for the twenty-four years of his professional career.

Ted Williams was often compared to John Wayne, the larger-than-life actor who had achieved a similar level of legendary and iconic status within American culture. I was fortunate enough to meet both men, albeit for short times. While traveling with my mother in the late 1970s, I met John Wayne in the Los Angeles Airport. He was dying of cancer, and could hardly speak because of the ravages to his throat. I felt bad for him because of the pain he must have been suffering, while at the same time realizing how lucky I was to have been in the presence of one of this country's most accomplished figures. Then in the late 1990s, while attending a meeting of the Hall of Fame's Veterans Committee in Florida, I met Ted Williams for the first time. It felt similar to the experience with John Wayne, but it was more sustained because circumstances allowed me to ask questions of Williams, rather than just shake his hand and say hello. Although Williams was also in declining health, as Wayne had been years earlier, the great hitter's voice remained loud and his mind remained sharp as he talked about old-time players and their deserving places in the Hall of Fame.

Based on just one conversation, I certainly can't say that I came to know Ted Williams. Unlike other authors and biographers who became friends or confidantes of the Boston Red Sox great, I did not write this book as someone who fully understood Williams on a personal level. Rather, I have used a variety of primary and secondary sources in trying to write an accurate, complete, and objective overview of his life, primarily as it pertained to baseball, while also touching upon his love of fishing and his heroic involvement in war. Along the way, I hope that I have shed some more light on those areas of his life and career that have not been discussed with as much depth, especially his underpublicized Mexican heritage and his often overlooked tenure as a major league manager. I hope that I have done justice to a fascinating and complicated man who excelled at almost anything he undertook and, through his zeal and commitment, became a truly epic American figure.

THE BOYHOOD OF A
HALL-OF-FAMER

Until the final few years of his life, most fans didn't even know that Ted Williams hailed from Mexican ancestry. How would they, considering his last name was Williams? His mother was born in Texas in 1893,[1] but was a mix of Mexican and French ancestry; part of her family hailed from the Mexican state of Chihuahua. While most of Williams' life and background would become well known—he became, after all, an American icon—his Mexican ancestry was one fact that remained relatively obscure throughout his life. He likely downplayed his heritage deliberately, so as to avoid any prejudice.

On August 30, 1918, at 2:20 in the afternoon, May Venzor Williams gave birth to a son, Teddy Samuel Williams, in the Sunshine Maternity Home, in San Diego, California.[2] A native of El Paso, Texas, May Venzor was one of nine children born to Natalia Hernandez and Pedro Venzor, who had married in 1888. Basque in origin, the Venzor family lived in the Mexican mining city of Hidalgo del Parral before moving to Texas to escape political unrest in Mexico. From Texas, the Venzors moved west to California, settling in Santa Barbara.[3]

During a stint as a commissioned lieutenant in the Salvation Army in Hawaii, May Venzor met and fell in love with Samuel Williams, who was on his way back to the United States after a military tour; the couple married in about 1915, shortly after Samuel's discharge from the military. Taking on the Williams name, she moved with Samuel to San Diego,[4] where they rented a series of apartments before settling down to buy a house.[5] While in San Diego, she spent much of her time continuing to work for the Salvation Army, trying to help poor people who needed assistance of various kinds, from alcoholics to unwed mothers to prostitutes.[6] She helped the impoverished throughout San Diego and even south of the border in Tijuana, earning her the nickname, "The Angel of Tijuana"[7]; some referred to her as "Salvation May."[8] She did almost everything for the charitable organization, from the selling of copies of *War Cry* (the Salvation Army's official publication) to the playing of a musical instrument—the cornet—in the Army band.[9]

The young Ted Williams felt a bit embarrassed by her association with the Salvation Army, as if such an occupation was something that lacked dignity, something not worthy of her time and effort. Yet her charitable work had an effect on Ted, who often gave his thirty cents lunch meal allowance to other children who came from needier backgrounds.[10] Her influence on Ted was considerable, given the dedication she displayed to the Salvation Army. May Williams spent much of her spare time, both at day and at night, often out as late as ten o'clock in the evening, contributing to one of the worthiest of American causes.

Ted's father, Samuel, consisted of a far different make-up than his mother. A product of English and Welsh ancestry,[11] Samuel hailed originally from the town of Ardsley, New York, located in an affluent region of Westchester County and one of the more desirable suburbs of New York City. He allegedly ran away from home at the age of sixteen to join the cavalry[12] and claimed to have fought with Teddy Roosevelt's Rough Riders during the war, but the accuracy of that assertion has come under question through further research. His admiration of Roosevelt reportedly influenced his decision to name his newborn son after the war hero, though Ted Williams himself claimed that his father had named him after a close friend and not the future president. (Williams' birth name was officially "Teddy," but he didn't like the moniker and later changed it to "Theodore." Most everyone called him "Ted.") Samuel served professionally in a series of occupations. He worked most notably as a photographer in a small shop above a restaurant,[13] a far cry from the non-profit world of the Salvation Army. For that, and other reasons, Samuel did not always fare well in his relationship with his wife. A quiet and introspective man, he possessed a hard exterior; he and his bride had differing interests and values, which caused them to struggle with their marriage, a difficulty that did not escape the awareness of their son. Samuel also spent a great deal of time away from the home. As a result of the family tension, Ted spent too much time alone while growing up in Southern California. And while Ted felt close to his mother, his relationship with his father was more distant, more aloof, partly because of the senior Williams' absence from the home, his considerable drinking, and his lack of interest in baseball. After Ted's formative years, Samuel Williams had little contact with his oldest son.

With his parents often away from home, other relatives began to exert more of an influence on young Ted's life, especially on his mother's side of the family. Ted made frequent visits to Santa Barbara, located about 200 miles from San Diego, where May Williams' younger sister, Sarah Diaz, looked after the boy on a regular basis.[14] Although Ted never learned to speak Spanish, he related to his Mexican relatives through other means. "Ted loved to hunt. He loved to fish," Diaz told Williams biographer and expert Bill Nowlin in a 2002 interview. "My father was a good fisherman, and all my brothers used to go out here on the wharf in Santa Barbara and fish."[15]

In addition to hunting and fishing, the Venzor side of the family exposed Ted to a sport not commonly followed throughout the United States: handball. Ted's uncle, Ernesto Ponce, was a world class handball player and a champion in three states (Arizona, New Mexico, and Texas). "Several of my . . . brothers played handball, [known in Spanish as] *pelota*," Ponce explained in an interview with Bill Nowlin. "When he was a young kid, Ted liked me. He'd always look at my hands and say, 'I want to be just like you.' These were the hands of a handball player. Big. Rough. We never talked baseball back then."[16] Ted enjoyed playing handball, becoming good at it, even if not at the same level as Ernesto and one of his other uncles, Pedro Jr.

Ted's visits to his mother's side of the family in Santa Barbara also fostered his interest in another sport. One of Ted's uncles, Saul Venzor, was an excellent athlete who played semipro baseball and excelled as a hard-throwing pitcher, both in the states and in Mexico. He also managed a semipro team, the Santa Barbara Merchants.[17] During Ted's trips to Santa Barbara, he often played baseball with Saul in the Venzors' large garden. They played catch and then took turns pitching and hitting against each other. Rather than just play recreationally, Saul made an effort to teach Ted about the game and how to improve his skills. Often demanding, Saul took a tough slant in coaching Ted, especially in regard to pitching. Yet, the approach worked. "Teddy would literally beg Saul to teach him how to pitch a baseball," said Manuel Herrera, one of Ted's cousins, who witnessed Saul's psychological methods of questioning the young boy's readiness and hunger. "Saul gave Ted more than just pitching lessons. He used a 'no-lose' attitude to build Ted's confidence and how to think and win. Not just to get the ball over the plate, but to think with your head and be aggressive."[18]

Saul also worked with Ted on his hitting, by challenging him to recognize and handle different kinds of pitches. According to another one of Ted's cousins, Frank Venzor, Saul had the ability to throw nineteen different pitches.[19] When Ted swung and missed, Saul and his brothers often teased him, sometimes to the point of drawing tears. Yet the approach seemed to work with Ted, who developed mental toughness and became determined to prove to Saul that he could succeed.[20]

Spurred on by his relationship with Saul, Ted developed a keen interest in baseball. Pure and simple, Ted loved the game, and he followed the sport with a passion. He didn't let his distance from large northeastern cities like New York or Philadelphia prevent him from stoking his interest in the major leagues. "I lived in San Diego, 3,500 miles from New York City," Williams told Hall of Fame Vice President Jeff Idelson during an interview in the year 2000. "Everything came out of New York. Of course I read the papers and the accounts of the games and certainly I knew of [Babe] Ruth and [Lou] Gehrig and [Al] Simmons and [Jimmie] Foxx. At the movies on Sundays or Saturdays, they might have some [clips] of major league games where somebody hit a home run, somebody drove in a winning run or somebody pitched a great game. And of course those were the players I got to know by name."[21]

In additions to Yankee greats like Gehrig and Ruth, Williams also followed the fortunes of star players from one of the other New York teams, the National League Giants, who featured Hall of Famers like Mel Ott and Bill Terry. Williams didn't restrict his interest to hitters. He also appreciated the achievements of several future Hall of Fame pitchers, including Philadelphia A's ace Robert "Lefty" Grove. "Of course, Carl Hubbell, Red Ruffing and Lefty Gomez, those names were big pitchers then."[22] Some of them would remain big names by the time that Ted made the major leagues, in time to face his boyhood heroes on the field.

As a young boy, Williams looked little like the supreme athlete that he would eventually become. Although he was one of the taller boys in his first-grade class, he sported an awkward-looking Dutch boy haircut that belied his lean physique. Bushy on top and on the sides, with bangs cut straight across his forehead, the unkempt hairstyle made the young Williams appear sissified. It also didn't help him when he played baseball, which he loved to do; the hair from his bangs often flopped over his eyes, affecting his eyesight whenever he took a turn swinging the bat. For this reason, even more than the unmanly appearance that it gave him, Williams fought to have his hair cut in a different manner, shorter and more streamlined.[23] Yet, as with many children of a young school age, Williams lost that battle with his parents—at least for awhile.

It was during grammar school that Ted first played in a competitive baseball game. That game took place in the Garfield School playground.[24] After games at Garfield, Ted typically stayed at the playground, waiting for an adult to come by and play a less structured game with him, a game known as "pepper." The premise of pepper was simple. Two players would stand a few feet apart, trying to keep the ball "alive" between them by bunting or lightly hitting the ball toward each other. Though a rudimentary game, it served to enhance the hand-eye coordination of its participants.

Ted's interest in baseball became obvious to his classmates, especially when he decided to carry a bat from classroom to classroom. "The reason I carried the bat was because it was a school bat," Williams told the Hall of Fame. "I got there early enough so I could be there to get the bat and the ball, and wait for the kids to play."[25]

While the young Williams spent most of his day at school and on the playground, he passed his nights in his family's modest home. Williams grew up in a house that was small and unimpressive. Given May Williams' work schedule, she had little time to tend to day-to-day upkeep, so its level of cleanliness failed to make up for its lack of size. The house had cost the Williams only about $4,000, and even then they had only been able to purchase the house through the assistance of another family, a large clan known as the Spreckles, who also lived in San Diego.

Yet, the home provided a boy like Ted, who enjoyed the outdoors, with some natural advantages. The Williams family happened to have a friendly next-door neighbor, an older gentleman named Chick Rotert.[26] He was now retired, but had previously worked as a game warden. Rotert often spent time showing young Ted pictures of lakes and streams where he had fished, some of his favorite locations on the West Coast. Rotert also showed him photographs of some of the larger, more impressive fish that he had caught. In addition, Rotert helped Ted select and buy his first fishing reel, which cost just under four dollars. Rotert essentially instructed Ted about the art of bass fishing, spurring an interest that Ted would possess for the rest of his life.[27]

The Williams' house provided Ted with another important outlet. Having lived in a string of rented apartments, the Williams moved into the undersized frame house five years after Ted was born.[28] Located at 4121 Utah Street, the small bungalow was situated only a block and a half from North Park playground, a terrific recreational park for a young boy with Ted's interests. With his mother often traveling to perform duties for the Salvation Army, Ted and his younger brother, Danny, usually had a decent amount of time to spend on their own. As a result, they frequently visited the park. While Ted couldn't hunt or fish at North Park, he could play ball there, sometimes for hours a day, where he usually worked on his swing until the lights of the park were finally shut off at around nine o'clock. And even then, he would return home and take some more swings against imaginary baseballs in his own back yard. That soon became Ted's obsession: swinging the bat from the left-hand side (even though he was naturally right-handed, he batted left-handed from the time he first picked up a bat), trying to hit his own tosses and lobs, refining his own skills of hitting at a young age.

Ted became friendly with the playground's director, a man who had once pitched in the minor leagues and continued to pitch at the semipro level. "Rod Luscomb was the playground director," Williams recalled in an interview with the Hall of Fame's Jeff Idelson.

> He was in charge of North Park playground, which was two blocks [actually a block and a half] from my house. He had been a great athlete himself in Arizona, where he went to school. He was really a frustrated old ballplayer. He wanted to play but was maybe not quite good enough at that time, but he was a hell of an athlete. He loved to be out on the playground and he certainly had a customer in me because I loved to be there too. I was a little better for my age than some kids and we had quite a few . . . a lot . . . of competitive little games among ourselves. He brought enthusiasm with his playing. He never really instructed me to do anything, except he played hard against me and I played hard against him. I was 17 and he was probably 28. He loved his work and I loved being on the playground. With him being so much better than I was, I liked that because it'd give me a chance to get up against a little better competition.[29]

Luscomb would often spend up to an hour at a time—sometimes longer—throwing batting practice to Williams, giving him an opportunity to fine-tune his swing.

Although Williams enjoyed working on his hitting skills by himself and with Mr. Luscomb, he also participated in games at North Park. He and his friends took part in both softball and baseball, often going as far as to play with old, damaged balls held together only by electrical tape. The boys, showing creativity along with their dedication, invented a game they called "Big League."[30] As part of that youthful creation, a player who hit a ball over a specific pipe earned a home run. Williams especially enjoyed playing Big League.

By his own estimate, Williams played ball at North Park for seven years. In one of the early highlights of his career, he hit a home run at the playground—a shot to straightaway center field. By then, Williams was already 15 years old, and the ball traveled nearly 300 feet, probably about 280 feet at the maximum.[31] While a home run of such length would pale in comparison to far more prodigious blasts in the future, it remained a memorable milestone for the young man who had become obsessed with hitting a baseball.

Williams carried his interest in hitting into his high school years. Hitting remained far more important to Ted than the classes that he took and the grades that he earned. "In school, I wasn't much of a student—a little below the other kids," Williams admitted in an interview with *Sports Illustrated*. "I never pushed myself at all. I always took subjects that I wouldn't have much homework in because I wanted more time for hitting. I took shop and things like that. I'm just lucky I didn't get my hands cut off."[32] In contrast to his success at hitting, Williams possessed no particular skill at shop.

Like many of the other boys attending Herbert Hoover High School, Williams needed to attend a tryout in order to make the varsity baseball team. That would prove to be an easy condition for Ted to meet. According to several witnesses on hand that day, Williams made an indelible impression during the first day of the tryout. The left-handed hitting Williams reportedly hit so many balls over the right-field fence and onto the roof of the school that Herbert Hoover's custodian ordered him to switch fields. That way, the school building would no longer become a landing pad for Williams' prodigious succession of practice home runs.

Clearly, Ted owned an advantage in work ethic that most of the other boys did not. By the time that he had enrolled at Herbert Hoover High School, he had already swung at literally thousands of pitches,[33] whether in practice or as part of pickup and organized baseball games. Williams' practice sessions, which became legendary in later years, might have struck some observers as boring, but only added to Ted's interest in the game. "I didn't even consider [it] practice," Williams told the Hall of Fame in the year 2000.

> The most fun I ever had in my life was if I was hitting a baseball and if I could hit one. . . . "Pow!" just like that, gee, that felt good to me. And as you get better at something you tend to like it a little more. I would run into somebody occasionally and all I could think was, "Boy, I hardly hit this guy." But the better the competition you are surrounded by, well, you start to get guys that are really tough [to hit]. But after a few times, he's not quite as tough as he was and that guy that used to be tough becomes easier to hit. And the practice, that was the most fun I ever did in my life and I was laughing because I got so much credit for it. It was the most fun I ever had.[34]

The coach of the Herbert Hoover Cardinals, a man named Wofford "Wos" Caldwell, took quick notice of Ted's rabid interest in hitting—even in the setting of the classroom. "That's all he wanted to do," said Caldwell. "Of course, the teachers would get upset every once in awhile. He'd sit there in his seat in the classroom and practice his swing rather than listen to what they were talking about."[35]

Although Williams had expressed his preference for hitting and had accumulated plenty of experience with the bat through his own work ethic and natural enjoyment of the game, Caldwell felt that Ted had the kind of physical build that was suited to pitching. Tall and thin, Williams seemed like a natural to work off the mound. A right-handed thrower, Ted was six feet, three inches tall, which was considered an ideal height for a pitcher. Yet, he weighed only about 146[36] to 148 pounds.[37] "I was a funny-looking kid, a string bean, a terribly scrawny-looking thing," Williams admitted in a 1955 interview with *Sports Illustrated*. "I certainly had no muscles. My mother used to get notes from the health office [saying], 'This kid is underweight; tonsils need checking, everything.'"[38]

Williams' rail-thin physique led some observers to wonder whether he was strong enough to hit and play the field on an everyday basis. So he split his time between pitching and playing positions like right field, third base, and first base, enjoying success in both areas of hitting and pitching. "Old ball players, especially old outfielders like to hear about their exploits on the mound," Williams informed the Hall's Jeff Idelson in 2000. "And the pitchers, they love to hear about any hit they got two years ago. Yeah, I was a pretty good little pitcher and I had good breaking stuff. I really think I had more fun in high school pitching than I did hitting. Hitting was still kind of tough to do, but if I could get my curve over and get my stuff over, I could get the guys out."[39] The right-handed Williams threw hard for a high school hurler, pitched strikes consistently, and featured an effective curveball and screwball, two pitches that were difficult for most high school hitters to handle.

In one of the highlights of his scholastic career, Williams pitched brilliantly in a tournament being held in Pomona. In one game against San Diego High School, Williams threw the ball masterfully. He struck out thirteen San Diego hitters, allowed only three hits, and earned a 6–1 victory for the Cardinals. He fared even better in another tournament game, supposedly striking out twenty-three batters (though this has never been verified through a newspaper account or boxscore) against Santa Monica High School. Williams also homered in that same game, marking perhaps the greatest all-around performance of his young career.[40]

Such performances motivated major league teams to begin scouting him. As a 15-year-old pitcher with his American Legion Post team in San Diego, Williams first drew interest from a major league scout. One of the first teams to learn about him was, coincidentally enough, the Cardinals—not the Herbert

Hoover Cardinals, but the St. Louis Cardinals of the National League. One of St. Louis' scouts, Herb Bennyhoven, came away so impressed by Williams' pitching that he invited him to a special tryout camp being hosted by the Cardinals. Williams attended the tryout camp, which was being held in Fullerton, not far from Ted's home. Unfortunately, the Cardinals didn't offer Williams a contract. As it turned out, they were far more interested in another amateur player, an outfielder named Lou Novikoff. Later known as the "Mad Russian," Novikoff would eventually make the major leagues, but would end up a huge disappointment. Novikoff would hit well, but only in the minor leagues, and not against the higher caliber of major league pitching.

Other teams showed interest in the young Williams. One of those teams, the Detroit Tigers, sent one of their scouts, Marty Krug, to Southern California to watch Williams play.[41] Krug felt Williams had talent, but also felt the youngster was too skinny and frail to play at more competitive levels. Krug advised Ted's mother, May, to discontinue the youngster's playing career out of concern for his safety. "When the Detroit scout saw what I looked like," Williams revealed to *Sports Illustrated,* "he told my mother, 'If you send that boy out and have him play professional baseball, it'll kill him.' Geez, my mother came home crying and everything. She was just sick."[42]

In actuality, Mrs. Williams had little reason to worry. Krug might have expressed more concern about the physical safety of the pitchers that Williams faced during his high school career. In his junior year, Williams damaged opposing pitchers to the tune of a whopping .583 batting average.[43] His performance in his senior season slipped a little, but he still managed to bat .403.[44] As a result of Williams' achievements with the bat, school officials awarded him a special statuette.

One of the Tigers' American League rivals also took a look at Williams. That team was the New York Yankees, who had been baseball's most dominant team in the 1920s and 1930s. One of their scouts liked Williams' potential at the plate, but sent a less-than-flattering report to Yankee owner Jacob Ruppert. In the letter, the scout praised Williams' talent as a hitter, but felt that he could be handled by smart pitching. In other words, the scout didn't feel that Williams had enough ability to play at the major league level.

Thankfully, the Yankees employed another scout who expressed a more favorable opinion of Williams. With Ted's high school eligibility coming to an end before his actual graduation from Herbert Hoover, Yankees scout Bill Essick tried to sign Williams in 1936. Essick was impressed with Williams' overall ability, both as a hitter and a pitcher. In addition to putting up his usually monstrous hitting numbers, Ted went 16–3 as a senior.[45] With such achievements planted in his mind, Essick wanted to offer the youngster a contract, but he would have to negotiate with his mother, who would have to grant permission for Ted to sign with a team. May Williams asked for $1,000, but Essick felt that was too much money and offered less. Mrs. Williams refused to budge, insisting on $1,000 for her son.[46] Essick wouldn't agree, Mrs. Williams again refused to lower her asking price, and the two sides stubbornly parted ways.

Ted had come close to fulfilling a dream—signing a contract to play in baseball's most successful and famous organization. Yet, a sum of money equaling less than $1,000 stood in Ted's way of completing his unlikely journey from Mexican roots through a lower class upbringing, to a potentially prosperous career doing what he loved to do best. And with his high school eligibility now expired, he couldn't even pursue that passion at the scholastic level. The beginning of Ted Williams' professional career, now in a state of limbo, would have to wait—for at least a little while longer.

NOTES

1. Bill Nowlin, "El Splinter Esplendido," *Boston Globe Magazine*, June 2, 2002, 15.

2. Ted Williams' birth certificate.

3. Nowlin, "El Splinter Esplendido," 15.

4. Ibid.

5. Ed Linn, *Hitter: The Life and Turmoils of Ted Williams* (New York: Harcourt Brace, 1993), 29–30.

6. Ibid.

7. Tim Wendel, *The New Face of Baseball: The 100-Year Rise and Triumph of Latinos in America's Favorite Sport* (New York: Rayo Publishing, 2003), 70.

8. Ed Linn, "The Kid's Last Game," *Sport*, February 1961, 52–63.

9. Ted Williams, with David Pietrusza, *Teddy Ballgame: My Life in Pictures* (Toronto: SportClassic Books, 2002), 10.

10. Linn, "The Kid's Last Game," 52–63.

11. Linn, *Hitter*, 29.

12. Ibid.

13. Ibid., 30.

14. Nowlin, "El Splinter Esplendido," 15.

15. Ibid.

16. Ibid., 17–18.

17. Ibid., 18.

18. Ibid., 18.

19. Ibid., 19.

20. Ibid., 19.

21. Interview with Ted Williams, conducted by Jeff Idelson of the National Baseball Hall of Fame, February, 2000.

22. Ibid.

23. Williams, with Pietrusza, *Teddy Ballgame*, 13.

24. Ibid., 16.

25. Interview with Ted Williams, conducted by Jeff Idelson of the National Baseball Hall of Fame, February, 2000.

26. Williams, with Pietrusza, *Teddy Ballgame*, 14.

27. Ibid.

28. Linn, *Hitter*, 29–30.

29. Interview with Ted Williams, conducted by Jeff Idelson of the National Baseball Hall of Fame, February, 2000.

30. Ibid.

31. Williams, with Pietrusza, *Teddy Ballgame*, 16.

32. Joan Flynn Dreyspool, "Ted Williams," *Sports Illustrated*, August 1, 1955, 29.

33. David Pietrusza, et al., eds., *Baseball: The Biographical Encyclopedia* (Kingston, NY: Total Sports, 2000), 1236.

34. Interview with Ted Williams, conducted by Jeff Idelson of the National Baseball Hall of Fame, February, 2000.

35. Dan Shaughnessy, "The Kid," *Boston Globe*, August 5, 1994, 76.

36. Linn, "The Kid's Last Game," 52–63.

37. Allen F. Davis, "Williams, Theodore Samuel (Ted)," in *The Scribner Encyclopedia of American Lives: Sports Figures*, ed. Arnold Markoe (New York: Charles Scribner's Sons, 2002), 501.

38. Dreyspool, "Ted Williams," 29.

39. Interview with Ted Williams, conducted by Jeff Idelson of the National Baseball Hall of Fame, February, 2000.

40. Williams, with Pietrusza, *Teddy Ballgame*, 19.

41. Ibid.

42. Dreyspool, "Ted Williams," 57.

43. Michael Seidel, *Ted Williams: A Baseball Life* (Chicago: Contemporary Books, 1991), 9.

44. Dan Riley, ed., *The Red Sox Reader* (Boston: Houghton Mifflin, 1991), 55.

45. Williams, with Pietrusza, *Teddy Ballgame*, 19.

46. Riley, *The Red Sox Reader*, 55.

THE PRO GAME

Many historians have speculated how Williams would have fared playing for the Yankees, with half of his games in Yankee Stadium, where the short porch in right field favored left-handed pull hitters. On paper, it would have seemed like a major advantage to a hitter like Williams, but he wasn't as sure about that possibility. "Well, there's probably been a lot of thought about that," Williams told the Hall of Fame, "just because Yankee Stadium was closer [in] right field and I was a pull hitter, you'd think boy, that'd work. [But] I want to tell you, I didn't get as many balls to pull in Yankee Stadium with a short fence as I did in Fenway [Park], where the fence is long [to right field]. At least I got good balls to hit [in Fenway]. You can be at Yankee Stadium all week before you get a ball [to hit]."[1]

In the meantime, the inability of the Yankees and May Williams to find common ground on a contract left Ted in an awkward position. With his eligibility to play baseball at Herbert Hoover High School having run out,[2] he no longer had a chance to showcase his playing skills to other big league scouts. The Williams' family was left with two options: Ted could continue to attend classes at Hoover and play baseball recreationally but not as part of organized competition, or he could transfer to another school.[3]

There existed other options besides the major leagues, as well. While most young players strove to play in the American or National leagues for one of the sixteen existing big league franchises, the West Coast offered a high-caliber league of its own. The Pacific Coast League (PCL), which featured franchises up and down the California coast, showed heavy interest in Williams. Although the PCL was considered a minor league, its talent level came close to approaching that of the major leagues. In fact, some scouts felt the PCL owned superior talent to the major leagues. Many players took the attitude that if they couldn't make a major league roster, the PCL represented their next best option. It was also a desirable destination for some players, because of its warm weather climates and generous salary structure. In some cases, PCL players made more money than their major league counterparts.

One of the Pacific Coast League teams, the Los Angeles Angels, liked Williams enough to sign him, but a personality conflict would prove to be a monumental stumbling block. Angels manager James "Truck" Hannah, who had once played with Babe Ruth on the Yankees, met with Ted's father, Samuel. The two men did not mesh well, with Samuel turned off by what he considered Hannah's arrogant attitude.[4] Once again, without parental permission, a contract with a professional team would not be signed.

Truck Hannah's personality conflict with Samuel Williams opened the door for another Pacific Coast League team, the transplanted San Diego Padres. (These were not the same San Diego Padres who would become a major league team in 1969.) The previous year, the Padres had actually played in Hollywood, California, and were nicknamed the "Stars." When Stars owner Bill Lane discovered that the city of Hollywood was going to double the amount of rent he would have to pay for his ballpark, he decided to move the team. That move had taken place in time for the newly named Padres to play in San Diego beginning in 1936.

The expansion Padres not only considered Williams a supreme talent, but they also liked his connection to Southern California. As a native of San Diego, Williams would provide the Padres with a local player who might bring extra fans to the ballpark.

In turn, May Williams liked the idea of her young son playing for the hometown team. That way, Ted would be able to live at home while with the Padres[5] and she would be able to attend many of his games. In addition, Bill Lane used his persuasive abilities to convince Mrs. Williams that she should permit her son to play professional ball. The fit between the 17-year-old Williams and the Padres seemed so natural that he ended up signing a contract in June of 1936, before his graduation from Herbert Hoover in February of 1937 and about two months into the Pacific Coast League season. Lane, who served as his own general manager, agreed to pay Williams $150 a month.[6] That kind of money paled in comparison to the kind of salaries that major league teams paid, but it was a sufficient starting point for Williams and his mother. They also appreciated the fact that Lane had including a full $150 payment for the month of June, even though

Ted had not officially signed until the month was nearly over.[7] That extra pay was considered Ted's bonus with the Padres.[8]

Williams joined an extremely talented team in San Diego. The Padres featured a host of former and future major leaguers, including Bobby Doerr at second base, Vince DiMaggio (the brother of Joe DiMaggio) in left field, and Cedric Durst (who had once played on the same team as Babe Ruth) in center field. The pitching staff included two excellent veterans in Herm Pillette and Frank Shellenback, the latter a smart left-hander who doubled as the Padres' manager. With such an excellent supporting cast in place, Williams' transition to professional baseball figured to be that much easier.

Yet, the Padres possessed so much talent that Ted did not start right away, always a frustrating predicament for a young player. Still, that was probably a good thing; Ted was only 17 years old and likely not ready to play a prominent role, at least not at the start of his professional career. As a result, manager Shellenback opted to let Ted break in slowly and decided to let the teenager make his debut in a pinch-hitting role. Williams entered a game in the late innings, facing Sacramento right-hander Cotton Pippen. His first at-bat would progress in something other than storybook fashion, as Ted struck out against the offerings of Pippen.

Shellenback also provided some opportunities for Williams to pitch, but the right-handed thrower lacked a powerful fastball and struggled against the excellent hitting featured in the Pacific Coast League. With his days as a pitcher numbered, Williams tried his hand almost exclusively as a position player. Williams played in a total of forty-two games during his rookie season and fared respectably. Exuding confidence, he hit .271 with 8 doubles and 2 triples, and certainly didn't embarrass himself in his first try against professional pitching. On the downside, the slender and underdeveloped Williams failed to hit with power—no home runs in his forty-two regular-season games (though he did hit one during the postseason). Still, Williams' performance started to draw the attention of Boston Red Sox general manager Eddie Collins, the Hall of Fame second baseman, who had made a scouting trip to San Diego during the second half of the season. Collins didn't offer Williams a contract, but liked the young hitter's fluid swing and intelligent approach at the plate.

Similarly, San Diego saw enough from Williams to bring him back for the 1937 season. The Padres lost their star second baseman, Bobby Doerr, who was purchased by Collins and the Red Sox, but brought back most of their other key players, including Durst. The Padres also added two key contributors to the mix, picking up second baseman Jimmie Reese (who would later gain fame as Babe Ruth's roommate) as a replacement for Doerr and finding a new catcher in George Detore. While Detore led the Pacific Coast League in hitting—an especially impressive achievement for a catcher—Williams upgraded his play substantially. More familiar with Pacific Coast League pitching in his second go-round, Williams overcame an early-season slump that saw him go hitless in 18 consecutive at-bats. By season's end, Williams improved his batting average by twenty points over his rookie year (from .271 to .291), collected 98 runs batted in (RBIs), and hit the first regular season home-runs of his professional career (23 to be exact, after having hit 1 home run during the 1936 PCL play-off series). Williams smartly took advantage of the dimensions at San Diego's ball-park, which featured a short distance to right field, where the outfield wall bordered the Pacific Ocean. Consciously trying to pull the ball at home, Williams deposited several pitches into the water beyond the right field fence. As Williams once said, "The ocean was only 100 yards from the plate."[9] In addition, Williams demonstrated that he had sufficient power to hit long balls in larger stadiums, as he delivered home runs in every one of the PCL's ballparks. With Williams and Detore forming the nucleus of the offense, the Padres finished a respectable third in the PCL's regular season standings.

The Padres only elevated their game in the postseason. Playing Sacramento in the first round of the Shaughnessy Playoffs, the Padres swept the series. That victory set up the finals for the championship of the league, a matchup of underdog San Diego against Portland. The Padres once again pulled off an upset, giving Williams his first league title in only his second season in the minor leagues. The championship capped off a terrific year of both individual and team success for the teenaged Williams.

Williams' batting prowess once again caught the eyes of major league scouts and managers, including representatives of the two Boston franchises in the major leagues. Eddie Collins and the Boston Red Sox showed interest for the second straight year, as did Casey Stengel, the manager of the Boston Braves. Collins proved to be the more aggressive of the two pursuers. One of Williams' batting practice sessions particularly impressed Collins, who asked Bill Lane to allow him to make the first bid on any claim for the young outfielder. The two executives eventually began negotiating over Williams. Lane wanted both cash and talent in return for the two-year Pacific Coast League veteran. Collins agreed to surrender two mediocre players in Dom Dallessandro and Al Niemiec and $35,000 in cash.[10] In what would prove to be one of the greatest transactions in the history of the franchise, the 19-year-old Ted Williams now belonged to the Boston Red Sox.

While Williams might have been expected to feel thrilled at the prospect of playing for a major league team, he harbored far different feelings about the move. He liked San Diego, where he played for a championship team, and didn't like the prospect of having to relocate all the way to the other coast, which was far away from the Southern Californian home and lifestyle to which he had become accustomed. He also didn't favor the prospect of joining a non-contending team in Massachusetts, where the Red Sox had forged a reputation as a mediocre team. Williams remained downtrodden about the deal—until he met the man responsible for making it.

Shortly after the announcement of the trade, the Red Sox arranged for Williams to meet with Collins. Ted came away extremely impressed. He liked Collins' gentlemanly demeanor; the Hall of Fame second baseman was both friendly and kind during their face-to-face session. "Eddie Collins was one of the great players and he was on the [Chicago] White Sox when they had their big scandal. He played with Joe Jackson," Williams recalled in an interview with the Hall of Fame. "Eddie Collins had played against Babe Ruth. He had played against all the great American League players then. In fact when Mr. [Tom] Yawkey bought the Red Sox, he said, 'If I can sign Eddie Collins to come with me, I'll buy 'em.' Well, he bought the club and got Eddie Collins with them. Wonderful man."[11] Williams quickly appreciated Collins' sense of baseball history and his knowledge of the game.

> He was one of the vice presidents [of the Red Sox], and he always wanted to talk about the Bambino or he wanted to talk about Gehrig or he wanted to talk [Al] Simmons possibly or he wanted to talk about [Robert] Moses Grove—Lefty Grove. So Eddie kept talking about the big players. Finally one day in our little house, I was sitting in the living room with Eddie Collins, and we'd been talking. I casually said, "Tell me about Joe Jackson [whom Collins had played with during his days with the White Sox]." Well I'll never forget what he did. He dropped his head when I said, "Joe Jackson," and he thought for maybe three or four seconds, then he looked up at the ceiling and said, "Boy, what a player he was." You could just see by his timing and his look and the way he said it that there was no question in his mind how good Joe Jackson was.[12]

During his first meeting with Ted, Collins also took time to explain to Williams that Red Sox owner Tom Yawkey was intent on building a winning team in Boston and replacing the legacy of mediocrity that had infiltrated the franchise since the sale of Babe Ruth to the rival New York Yankees. Unlike some other owners who were more concerned with profit and loss, Yawkey placed winning higher on the priority list—and was willing to spend money to achieve the goal. Within a short span of time, Williams realized his fortune in having an owner as generous as Yawkey. "It's probably the greatest break I ever got," Williams informed the Hall of Fame, "[that] I got to play for Mr. Yawkey; he was an absolute gem of a guy. He was one of the truly great owners in baseball because he thought of the players a lot, he thought of ways to help them. It was a dream [for him] from the time he was old enough to realize what 35 million bucks was. He said, 'I'm going to buy a ball club,' and he stayed with it the rest of his life."[13]

Although Williams often praised Yawkey and seemed to enjoy a solid relationship with his boss, the two men never became as close as a superstar athlete might with a team's owner. In later years, Yawkey would develop a much closer friendship with Williams' successor in left field, Carl Yastrzemski.[14] So why the subtle tension between Yawkey and Williams? Some writers and observers have speculated that it may have had something to do with their different backgrounds and philosophies.[15] While Yawkey had grown up in a rich household and had little exposure to the lower classes, Williams had been raised from more modest beginnings, influenced by a mother who performed charity work for poor people. In addition, Williams had worked hard to become a great player, while Yawkey had inherited all of his wealth, providing him with a more leisurely lifestyle.[16]

With Yawkey writing the checks, Collins explained to Williams that if he were to make the Red Sox major league roster in 1938, he would earn $3,000 as a rookie, and a raise to $4,500 in his second season.[17] While those salaries might not have been high for a major league player in the late 1930s, they were far better figures than the $200 per month (or about $1,900 for a full season) that Williams was earning as a second-year member of the Padres. Now it was up to Ted to make the Red Sox roster during the spring of 1938, so that he could begin earning the kind of money that Collins had promised.

In 1938, Williams attended his first major league spring training, joining the Red Sox at their preseason camp in Sarasota, Florida. The cross-country trip from California to Florida proved difficult, especially when California was hit with a massive flood. As a result of the weather conditions, Williams couldn't contact Bobby Doerr by telephone; Doerr, under instructions from Red Sox general manager Eddie Collins, was supposed to pick Williams up in San Diego and accompany him by car to Florida, so as to make sure that the unpredictable Williams stayed out of trouble.[18] Doerr eventually reached Williams by ham radio, but by then, it was too late for the two men to meet in the Imperial Valley. Instead, Doerr advised Williams to make his way out of the flooded area by driving to El Paso, where they would meet on their way to Florida.[19] To make the trip, Williams had to borrow $200.[20] It was an early sign that spring training would run less than smoothly for the former Pacific Coast League star.

When Doerr arrived in El Paso, he found not only Williams waiting for him, but also Babe Herman, an aging but colorful and talkative outfielder who had played for the Tigers in 1937. The three hopped on a Pullman train to Florida, but Ted had to cut the train ride short when he came down with the flu, which forced him to stay over in New Orleans. As a result, Williams didn't reach the Red Sox spring training camp until ten days after his scheduled arrival.[21]

When Ted did finally land in Florida, he found himself embroiled almost immediately in a dispute. Wearing a loose fitting shirt that was not tucked into his pants, which made him look sloppy, Williams was called a "busher" by a man he had never previously met. Williams couldn't let the insult go without a sarcastic reply of his own. Williams didn't realize it at the time, but the man who had criticized him was none other than Red Sox manager Joe Cronin, their former shortstop and a Boston icon.

Williams' tendency at making unfavorable first impressions continued when he met Red Sox owner Tom Yawkey. "Don't look so worried, Tom," Williams said informally after being introduced to Boston's chief executive.[22] He followed up the informality with an immediate dose of brashness. "[Jimmie] Foxx and me will take care of everything."[23]

Although the Red Sox regarded Williams almost as highly as he regarded himself, the youngster faced a daunting task; trying to crack an excellent starting outfield. The Red Sox already featured three good everyday outfielders in Joe Vosmik, Doc Cramer, and Ben Chapman. To make Boston's starting lineup, one of the three regulars would have to fall victim to injury, or Williams would have to play so well that Eddie Collins would feel motivated to trade one of his veteran starting outfielders.

Neither development would take place. None of the starting outfielders came down with an injury, and Williams did not play well in spring training exhibition games. It didn't help matters that the three veteran outfielders didn't treat Williams kindly, resenting the fact that he might provide a challenge to their status as starters. They rode him hard, giving him what might be considered the typical "razzing" that veterans heaped on rookies during that era. Rather than ignore the veterans' barbs, Williams responded by unveiling his arrogant side. In addition to the three starting outfielders, Williams annoyed many of the other Red Sox veterans by displaying a haughty attitude. He acted like an established veteran who was already guaranteed a position on the team, rather than like an unproven rookie who was making an effort to show respect toward the older players on the team.

As the Red Sox prepared to make their first road trip of spring training—a jaunt to Tampa—Williams found out that he would not be accompanying the

Red Sox veterans on the team bus. The Red Sox had decided to send him to Daytona Beach, where their minor leaguers trained during the spring. At that point, Williams realized he would not be traveling to Boston for the start of the regular season.

Red Sox management informed Williams that he had not made the team and would instead start the season playing in the minor leagues, for the Red Sox top-ranked affiliate at Class Double-A Minneapolis, a franchise in the American Association. Even the news of a demotion failed to shake Williams' extreme confidence and cockiness. Shortly after learning about his one-way ticket to Minneapolis, Williams supposedly told the three starting outfielders that he would return soon and would eventually make more money than all of them combined. Williams also delivered a promise, one that the writers managed to quote him on for print purposes. "I'll be back," Williams said. "I'll be back and I'll drive those old buzzards clear out of baseball."[24] It was a nearly unprecedented lack of humility and tact being shown by a raw teenager who had yet to play in an actual major league game.

Unhappy with the Red Sox decision not to carry him on the twenty-five-man major league roster, Williams initially allowed his disappointment over a spring training demotion to affect his play in the minor leagues. He started slowly with the Minneapolis Millers, sometimes failing to hustle on the field and making himself a verbal target of the local fans. Feeling that he belonged in the major leagues, Williams annoyed teammates and coaches with his attitude and immaturity; at one point in the season, Millers manager Donie Bush threatened to quit because of Williams' unprofessional approach.[25] Yet, team owner Mike Kelley refused to rid the Millers of Williams, who was hitting the ball passionately after an inauspicious beginning. In essence, Kelley told Bush that he wouldn't part ways with a .360 hitter like Williams, but wouldn't stand in the way if *Bush* wanted to leave. With the message delivered, Bush stayed, and Williams continued to batter American Association pitching. Williams went on to forge a set of impressive statistics in his first season with the Millers, batting .366 with 43 home runs and 142 RBIs, all improvements over the numbers that he had posted the previous season with San Diego. More impressively, Williams led all American Association players in each of these three most recognized offensive categories, earning him the league's Triple Crown. That he accomplished the feat at the age of 20 only cemented his growing reputation as a top-notch major league prospect.

Several circumstances combined to make Williams' season in Minnesota a productive one. As he did in San Diego, Williams seized the advantage provided by his home ballpark. The Millers played in cozy Nicollet Park, where the distance down the right field line measured only 279 feet. The length to right center field also provided Williams with an easy target, one that was tailored to his pull-hitting style. Defensively, the relatively small amount of acreage in right field eased Williams' fielding burden. Donie Bush played Williams in right field, giving an inexperienced and sometimes clumsy outfielder less ground to cover defensively than he would have needed in left field. That allowed Ted to expound most of his energy at the plate, where he preferred to devote the majority of his attention.

Williams was also aided by the influence of his manager in Minneapolis. Although Bush often grew frustrated with Williams' temperament, and sometimes dreaded watching him stumble through the outfield where he made frequent mistakes and misjudgments, Bush usually managed to hold his temper with Ted and succeeded in making a connection with the young phenom. A patient hitter throughout his professional career—he led his league in walks five times in the minors and majors—Bush confirmed Williams' own belief in displaying discipline at the plate. As a result, Williams began to fully comprehend the importance of patience as a hitter, the refusal to swing at bad pitches, and the insistence on hitting good ones. Williams listened to Bush, in part because he genuinely liked his manager, a friendly old-time baseball man who was revered by most of the other players and coaches on the Minneapolis team.

Another favorable factor in Minneapolis involved Ted's batting coach. It was Hall-of-Famer Rogers Hornsby, arguably the greatest right-handed hitter in the game's history and a proponent of selective, patient hitting at the plate, a philosophy that emphasized the importance of swinging only at good pitches. Williams quickly grasped this approach, helping him develop a keen sense of the strike zone. As a manager, Hornsby had often struggled in his ability to communicate with players, but on this occasion he registered with Williams. "Well, you know Hornsby was a tough guy and he had problems with ownership and he was a cantankerous old guy," Williams said in an interview with the Hall of Fame. "And boy I loved him. He treated me just like I was a young son that he was having fun with. He was just absolutely great."[26]

Williams' regular conversations with Hornsby about the art of hitting proved beneficial, even if Ted didn't always concur with Hornsby's philosophies. "He didn't really work on the mental approach with me as much as just talking about hitting," said Williams.

> His understanding [of] how he hit so well, I didn't agree with even at a young age. For example, he said if the ball's outside, I step outside, then I hit 'em. Ball inside, then I hit the ball to right field. You can't do that really 'cause you don't know where the ball is or what

it is until it gets ten feet from the plate. You can't make that adjustment that fast. So, I listen to [Hornsby]; I tried to listen to everybody, because sometimes they'll say something that sounds all right and gee I didn't realize that. Then I might go out and try that and it still didn't do me any good. Then I just kind of forget about it. But once in awhile I'd get a little kind of something [that would register with me]. I hear somebody say [about me], boy, he's got quick wrists. Well, I didn't know if that was real bad or real good or bad or what, but he noticed that. He thought [I'm] good and I thought to myself, "He thinks I'm quick, now wait until the next time he sees me." It was little things like that you pick up and you listen to and you try things that you think might help you.

For Williams, the efforts to improve involved a process of four steps. "Well certainly, to improve, you got to be observant, to improve you got to be listening, to improve you got to experiment. Then you have to decide whether that's good or bad. You keep the good and throw the other stuff away. You separate the good from the bad, keep the good."[27] By observing, listening, experimenting, and separating, Williams continually lifted his skills in hitting a baseball.

Williams also found fortune in having quality teammates. Although the Millers finished the season with a mediocre record just above .500, they featured a number of future major leaguers. In addition to Williams, players like Stan Spence, Jim Tabor, and "Broadway" Charlie Wagner—all future major leaguers—also dotted Minneapolis' roster. With high-caliber players surrounding him, Williams profited from the big league atmosphere that emerged in the clubhouse and on the playing field.

And then there was the surrounding environment provided by the state of Minnesota. Williams liked the Twin Cities and the neighboring areas. His level of contentment with the region was reflected in his on-field performance, which bordered on the brilliant. Although the Millers did not play in the major leagues, they provided one of the best settings possible for a minor league prospect like Williams.

Williams' single-season performance for Minneapolis convinced Red Sox management that it could start to break up its veteran major league outfield. After the 1938 season, the Red Sox traded Ben Chapman, one of their outfield mainstays, to the Cleveland Indians. The deletion of Chapman meant that the Red Sox would have a new right fielder in 1939, with Williams and a little known outfielder named Red Nonnenkamp providing the competition. Like Williams, Nonnenkamp batted from the left side of the plate, which meant that the two hopefuls would not be able to platoon with each other in 1939. One or the other would win the right field job, but not both.

The spring of 1939 brought Williams another adventuresome cross-country journey. As he made his way to Florida, Williams again came down with a severe cold. Already plagued by persistent respiratory problems, the illness forced Williams to interrupt his lengthy trip. He stopped off in New Orleans, where he remained for three days in an effort to recuperate. Finally feeling better, Ted completed the last leg of his long ride to Sarasota.[28]

During spring training in 1939, Red Sox second baseman Bobby Doerr, a teammate of Williams with the San Diego Padres, approached Ted and offered him a quick preview of what he could expect to see from one of the Red Sox veterans, "Wait 'till you see Foxx hit,"[29] Doerr said, referring to first baseman Jimmie "Double X" Foxx. The future Hall of Famer was generally regarded as Boston's most intimidating batsman. In no mood to express awe or reverence for another hitter, Williams provided Doerr with a classic reply. "Wait 'till Foxx sees *me* hit!"[30]

The Red Sox felt confident that Williams could hit, but they weren't as sure about his defensive abilities—or his temper. After missing a pop-up during an exhibition game in Atlanta, Ted picked up the ball and threw it out of the ballpark. At this point Williams was starting as a right fielder, since Joe Vosmik was established in left field, and right-fielder Ben Chapman has been traded. Manager Joe Cronin, who already had experienced Williams' immaturity upon the youngster's arrival in Sarasota, fined him $50 for the indiscretion. Seemingly never at a loss for words, Ted responded with an amusing counter-proposal. "I'll pay you $50 for every one I throw out," said Williams, "if you'll pay me $50 for every one I hit out."[31]

Later in the spring, Williams participated in a preseason exhibition in Worcester, against the collegiate team at Holy Cross. In what amounted to his debut in the Commonwealth of Massachusetts, Williams blasted a grand slam in the first inning.[32] The spectators at Fitton Field had enjoyed a brief glimpse of the kind of hitting display that they would witness many times over the next two decades.

With spring performances like the one in Worcester, Williams beat out Red Nonnenkamp for the starting right field position with Boston. After playing three seasons in the Pacific Coast League and the American Association, Williams had finally cracked the major league barrier. He would now wear the same uniform sported by a quartet of the city's best and most famous players: Jimmie Foxx, Bobby Doerr, Joe Cronin, and Lefty Grove. The latter was the Red Sox staff ace and one of the legends that Williams had admired as a youngster. Grove was no longer just a player for Williams to worship from afar. He was now a teammate. Fulfilling a dream, Ted Williams had arrived in the major leagues.

NOTES

1. Interview with Ted Williams, conducted by Jeff Idelson of the National Baseball Hall of Fame, 2000.

2. Riley, *The Red Sox Reader*, 55.

3. Correspondence with Bill Nowlin, November 17, 2003.

4. Williams, with Pietrusza, *Teddy Ballgame*, 20.

5. Correspondence with Bill Nowlin, November 17, 2003.

6. Pietrusza, *Baseball*, 1236.

7. Correspondence with Bill Nowlin, November 17, 2003.

8. Williams, with Pietrusza, *Teddy Ballgame*, 20.

9. Curt Smith, *Storied Stadiums: Baseball's History Through Its Ballparks* (New York: Carroll and Graf, 2001), 331.

10. Williams, with Pietrusza, *Teddy Ballgame*, 22.

11. Interview with Ted Williams, conducted by Jeff Idelson of the National Baseball Hall of Fame, 2000.

12. Ibid.

13. Ibid.

14. Howard Bryant, *Shut Out: A Story of Race and Baseball in Boston* (New York and London: Routledge, 2002), 65.

15. Ibid.

16. Ibid.

17. Williams, with Pietrusza, *Teddy Ballgame*, 22.

18. Ed Linn, "Growing Up With Ted," *Sport*, February 1966, 56.

19. Ibid.

20. Williams, with Pietrusza, *Teddy Ballgame*, 27.

21. Linn, "Growing Up With Ted," 56.

22. Ibid.

23. Ibid.

24. Lee Greene, "Ted Williams' Ten Greatest Days," *Sport*, June 1959, 26.

25. Pietrusza et al., *Baseball*, 1236.

26. Interview with Ted Williams, conducted by Jeff Idelson of the National Baseball Hall of Fame, 2000.

27. Ibid.

28. Williams, with Pietrusza, *Teddy Ballgame*, 26.

29. Smith, *Storied Stadiums*, 170.

30. Ibid.

31. Pietrusza et al., *Baseball*, 1236.

32. Riley, *The Red Sox Reader*, 55.

DONNING THE SOX

On April 20, 1939, the Red Sox opened their season on the road against the rival New York Yankees, who were scheduled to start their ace right-hander, Red Ruffing. Manager Joe Cronin inserted Williams into the starting lineup as his right fielder and sixth-place hitter. Settling into the batter's box before a crowd of 30,278 fans at Yankee Stadium, the skinny kid from San Diego eyed Ruffing, one of the game's best pitchers. Not so surprisingly, Ruffing overmatched Williams, giving him an unwelcome start to his major league career. "First game, first time, I struck out," Williams told the Hall of Fame without embarrassment.

> That first time Ruffing was sneaky fast. He threw with a little *umph!* Boy! There it was! If you didn't realize this guy could throw and do so with less motion and effort and excitement—it was by you! My first key on him was—the first thing I forever had to be conscious of was this guy is sneaky and he is faster than he looks. Now I've run into quite a few pitchers that I thought were faster than they looked. One was Billy Pierce [of the Chicago White Sox]. A little guy but just the fact that he wasn't big and how hard he threw, you had to say, "He's faster than he looks, he's faster than he looks!" [Dizzy] Trout was another big strong guy who didn't throw a lot of effort into it but boy, he could throw the ball too. He was another one. There were other guys that could throw a little harder than you thought they could throw. But once you struck out once or twice against them, and it was *Umph!* and by you, then you'd have to come to that end result and say, "Boy, he's faster than he looks."[1]

Yes, he did play some defense as well. Ted displays his throwing form prior to a game at Fenway Park. After Williams' first season in Boston, the Red Sox switched his defensive position from right to left field. *National Baseball Hall of Fame Library, Cooperstown, N.Y.*

In spite of that first strikeout at the hands of Ruffing, Williams didn't lack in confidence, a trait that was noticed by at least one of his Red Sox mates. "One of my teammates kind of thought I was a little bit cocky," said Williams.

> I didn't mean to be but apparently I acted that way. He came all the way down from the end of the dugout, I could see him coming and I couldn't believe what he'd want being up in our end of the dugout. I was up by the water fountain and the bat rack and here he comes right for me. Then he says to me, what do you think of the big leagues? Well, I'd been up . . . and I'd struck out . . . and I had to think it was pretty tough. I gave him a little sass but I also said this, I said, "I *know* I can hit that guy." Well, I later proved that I did hit 'em pretty good.[2]

Williams fared much better his second time up. Batting in the fourth inning as the Red Sox trailed the Yankees, 1–0, Williams clanked a ball off the right-center field wall at Yankee Stadium, resulting in a clean double. It was a memorable first hit—a 407-foot blast that resulted in extra bases, occurring in one of baseball's most famed ballyards, and coming against a future Hall-of-Famer. It didn't matter much that Williams would endure hitless at-bats his next two times up, that he struck out twice in his debut, or that the Red Sox would lose the game, 2–0; Williams, with a resounding double, had broken in stylishly on one of the game's great stages.

The box score from Williams' first game reveals a "Who's Who of the American League" for the 1930s. In addition to Williams and Ruffing, seven other Hall-of-Famers participated in that Opening Day game at the Stadium. For the Red Sox, there was first baseman Jimmie Foxx (batting third), shortstop-manager Joe Cronin (batting cleanup), second baseman Bobby Doerr (batting seventh, just ahead of Williams), and Lefty Grove, who handled the pitching chores. For the Yankees, Joe DiMaggio was in center field (batting cleanup), Lou Gehrig at first base (batting fifth), and Bill Dickey behind the plate (batting sixth). In an intriguing footnote, it marked the only game in which Williams and Gehrig both played.[3]

The next day, Williams made his first appearance at Fenway Park, located in downtown Boston. Playing against the famed Philadelphia A's, managed by Connie Mack, Williams singled once in 5 at-bats. Like he had done in his first game, Williams managed to pick up one hit in his debut at one of the eastern seaboard's most famed ballparks.

Later in that series against the A's, Williams achieved another milestone. On April 23, he belted his first major league home run. The long ball highlighted a huge day for Williams, who also banged out a double and two singles in going

4-for-5. He also drove in 3 runs of Boston's 8 runs. In spite of 12–8 loss to the A's, Williams had succeeded in putting together his first standout game as a member of a major league roster.

Williams seemed comfortable hitting at Fenway Park that day, but playing in Boston's home park still posed an adjustment for a young player like Williams, who had grown up in a far different geographic region and climate. "Don't forget Fenway Park was the furthest place from where I lived in San Diego," Williams told the Hall of Fame. "Here I am [coming from the] Southwest and there they are North. I didn't want to go there. Sure I knew where Boston was but I never been there and they had snow and they had cold and they had longer periods of colds than San Diego. I never did like to play in cold weather much. [But] you get used to playing."[4]

The cooler weather of the Northeast forced Williams to undergo at least one kind of transition. The prospects of facing major league pitching, however, did not. Unlike many rookies who confess to being awestruck over their first trip through the major leagues, Williams expressed no such fears or feelings of intimidation. When interviewed by sportswriters—and there were plenty of them, with seven Boston newspapers covering the team—Williams made several blunt observations. For example, he saw no blinding fastballs or overwhelming curveballs. Rookie hitters were supposed to express reverence for opposing pitchers, regardless of how well they performed at the plate. Such was not the case for Williams, whose brutal honesty made some of the writers and many of his teammates cringe.

When a writer asked questions of Williams, he didn't hesitate to think about what the diplomatic response might be; he spoke freely, expressed what was on his mind, often used profanity, and often disagreed with the writer's premise. Williams' willingness to contradict writers made him seem almost confrontational. From a veteran, such a tone might have been more understandable, but coming from an unproven rookie, it was more like baseball heresy.

Not surprisingly, Williams quickly established himself as somewhat of a contrarian with writers and teammates. His general attitude in conducting interviews annoyed some of the older scribes, but his non-clichéd responses came across as refreshing to another portion of the baseball writers. For that reason, he became a popular figure and writing subject of the Boston press, which dubbed him "The Splendid Splinter." (The nickname made sense, given Williams' 6-foot, 3-inch, 168-pound frame. Williams preferred to call himself "The Kid," which he began doing early in his Red Sox career. Williams also liked being referred to as "Teddy Ballgame," a practice that started when the young son of a Boston photographer, asked to name the ballplayer he most wanted to meet at Fenway Park, responded by saying, "Teddy . . . Teddy Ballgame.") Williams also developed a good early relationship with the Boston fans. According to reports, he treated fans—especially children—with kindness and respect, which helped make him a fan favorite.[5] When fans gave him a rousing ovation for hitting a home run or executing a fine catch in the outfield, he acknowledged the cheers with a friendly—and unusual—tip of the cap. Employing a unique style, Williams lifted the cap by its button rather than by its bill, tipping it for his newly discovered friends at Fenway.[6]

Williams also found some allies in the Boston clubhouse. One of the most influential was Red Sox coach Hugh Duffy. Although only 5 feet, 7 inches tall, Duffy had forged an impressive resume during his many years in baseball, which dated back to the nineteenth century. A major league star who had batted .440 in 1894, he later became a mainstay for the Red Sox, helping form one of the game's best outfields in the early part of the twentieth century. Long since retired, Duffy now played the role of baseball sage, passing along the wisdom compiled through vast experience in the game. Impressed by Williams' swing and general approach to hitting, Duffy constantly reminded Ted of the importance of maintaining good form at the plate.[7] He didn't want Williams to abandon that form in trying to hit for more power, but felt that the power would come as long as he maintained the proper form.

Williams also found support from his manager, which was somewhat surprising given their uneasy encounters in spring training. Joe Cronin showed enormous confidence in Williams by batting him ahead of the more experienced Bobby Doerr, and by occasionally batting him right behind Jimmie Foxx, the team's most feared hitter. Cronin also asked players and coaches to voice words of encouragement to Williams, whose young ego needed a helpful massage from time to time.

Williams appreciated having an offensive-minded manager like Cronin on his side. "It was a dream come true for a young kid that thought hitting was everything," Williams told the Hall of Fame, "and Cronin was a good hitter."

> He always was talking about the hitting [on the team] and never about the fielding and never about the pitching. Cronin could always sum up everything fast; for example he said [that when you face a] fastball pitcher, make him come down [in the strike zone]. And if we had [to face] a sinkerball pitcher that day and [he threw] a curve ball in the dirt, make him come up. Now there's ways to make a pitcher appear to be throwing up a little and ways to make a high fast ball pitcher appear to be not as fast or he gets the ball down lower. Now, if I'm way up close to him [in the batter's box], [and he's throwing] a fastball and . . . you know that the angle of the ball

is going down, so when it's up, it's definitely high. So you can help yourself that way a little bit by getting back further [in the batter's box]. The same way with the sinkerball [pitcher], get up closer to him because everything will be up a little bit more.[8]

With friends like Duffy and proponents like Cronin helping to keep him centered, Williams enjoyed a rookie season that could be categorized as nothing less than a rousing success. The Fenway freshman concluded his first year with a .327 batting average, 31 home runs, and 145 RBIs. Williams showed unusual power for a young man with such a slender build, becoming the first player to hit a home run completely out of Briggs Stadium in Detroit.[9] Even more impressively, Williams clubbed seven home runs into the right field bleachers at Fenway Park, one of the most difficult places to reach home distance in the American League. Only a small handful of five players had previously shown such prodigious right field power at Fenway Park,[10] which featured far more favorable dimensions in left field.

In 1940, the Red Sox made an effort to shorten the right-field dimensions, a move that figured to help Williams. The Sox decided to put up a bullpen beyond the right-field fence and in front of the bleachers, thereby bringing the right-field wall closer to home plate. The change made the distance to right center field 380 feet, a far more reasonable length for a left-handed power hitter. Some fans and writers started referring to the bullpen area as "Williamsburg," cementing the connection of the distance change to the impact that it had on Williams.

The Red Sox also made another change, one that was also specifically tailored to assist Williams. Manager Joe Cronin switched him from right field to left field, so that he would not have to deal with the sun field at Fenway Park. From right field, an outfielder looked directly into the sun, having to deal with an unusual amount of brightness and direct light. The Red Sox didn't want Williams to hurt his eyes from the excessive glare of right field.

Another alteration figured to ease Williams' burden in the outfield. The Red Sox brought a promising youngster named Dom DiMaggio to the major leagues in 1940, playing him in all three outfield positions. An accomplished defensive outfielder with an abundance of speed and range, DiMaggio would make fifty-nine appearances in center field in 1940 before playing center on a full-time basis in 1941, cutting down on the amount of territory that Williams needed to cover, especially toward the left-center-field gap.

In 1940, Williams batted .344, a seventeen-point improvement over his rookie season, and led the American League with 134 runs scored. Each of the Red Sox starting infielders (not including the catcher's position) reached the 20–

home-run plateau. From a statistical standpoint, the Red Sox held the appearance of a pennant-winning team. In actuality, they finished a disappointing fourth, a nonfactor in the American League title race.

Why did the Red Sox fall short? Some critics targeted the pitching, while a few pointed in the direction of Williams. Strangely, Williams' power numbers fell off from his rookie season, despite the shortening of the distance to the right field wall. In trying to account for the falloff, some Red Sox observers criticized Williams for what they perceived as a failed work ethic. Upset by the insinuations that he didn't work sufficiently hard, Williams became angered and reacted by saying that he would prefer not to be a ballplayer but serve as a fireman instead. (On the team's next trip into Chicago, White Sox players wore fire helmets as a way of poking fun at Williams' rash pronouncement.)[11] Williams' impulsive declaration spurred on further boos from the fans and even more community criticism, producing a contentious relationship with the media and fans throughout Boston. Williams eventually vowed that he would never tip his cap toward the fans again.

While Williams and the fans had started to sour on each other, his relationship with the Boston media also began to deteriorate. One writer described Williams as an "abnormal youth" because of his decision not to return home to visit his mother during the off-season. The criticism stung Williams, who resented personal attacks from a media base that he considered intrusive. He didn't like writers who pried into his private life, especially during the winter months.

Several Boston area writers, including Austen Lake of the *Boston Evening American*, began to weave feelings of disapproval toward Williams into their columns, making the young star a frequent target of ridicule. Yet, Lake's harsh portrayals of Williams paled in comparison to those of another local writer. Dave Egan, a columnist for the *Boston Record*, carried his scathing criticism of Williams to such an extreme that he seemed hell-bent on portraying Williams as Public Enemy No. 1. A Harvard graduate and a lawyer, Egan was an intelligent man and a talented writer, but he had his vices. He drank heavily, sometimes so much so that another writer would have to be called in to write his column.[12] Known as "The Colonel," Egan developed such a severe dislike of Williams that he once referred to the Red Sox star as the "inventor of the automatic choke."[13] Even when Williams played well, Egan found areas for criticism, often venturing into the realm of nitpicking.

In spite of the problems that arose during his sophomore season, Williams did fulfill a small dream during one of the lighter moments of the summer. With the Red Sox losing a lopsided game in Detroit, Joe Cronin decided to allow Williams to pitch the final innings. Not having pitched since his minor league days, Williams took a turn against major league hitters. He pitched two innings, allowing one run and three hits. In the brightest spot of his unexpected relief stint, Williams struck out Tigers slugger Rudy York on a big, breaking sidearm curveball. It was the highlight of his first—and only—pitching appearance in the major leagues.

The start of the 1941 season, his third in the big leagues, brought more trouble Ted's way. He failed to report to spring training on time, mostly because he was upset with the Red Sox salary offer of $12,500, which fell into the category of "take it or leave it." He remained out of sight—and out of touch. The day after the start of training camp, Williams finally called Eddie Collins and explained his absence by telling the general manager that he had been hunting wolves in the woods of Minnesota and had lost track of time and the dates on the calendar. Trying to sound apologetic, Williams said he would begin driving to Florida immediately.

Williams' unexcused late arrival in preseason camp spurred insinuations that he intentionally shunned spring training because of his dislike for it. Such suggestions only continued later in his career. "They say I try to avoid spring training," Williams proclaimed in a 1955 interview with *Sports Illustrated*. "The only thing I do know is, of all the players in the big leagues, I'll bet I've played more spring training games than anybody around. I don't like to play them just to be playing. . . . I know I can get into shape better in my own spring training in ten days, doing what I want to do, just as long as I want to do it. . . . In three weeks, I can be in pretty good shape. I do a lot of calisthenics and that type of thing in the offseason."[14]

After making his late arrival in the Sunshine State, another problem arose during the spring of '41. Williams chipped his ankle bone, affecting his timetable for the start of the regular season. Williams started the season slowly, appearing mostly as a pinch hitter, and didn't begin to play regularly until late April.

By the middle of May, Williams' injured foot had reached nearly 100 percent health. On May 15, he started a twenty-three-game hitting streak; he would bat .487 during the stretch. At about the same time that Williams embarked on his streak, Joe DiMaggio started the most famed stretch of his career. He picked up hits in each game, first for ten straight games, then twenty, then thirty. As the streak moved into the thirty- to forty-game range, the baseball world began to pay strict attention to DiMaggio's every move. During Red Sox home games, Williams would find out DiMaggio's progress from the scoreboard operator, who was situated inside the left field wall, and pass the information along to Joe's brother, Red Sox center fielder Dom DiMaggio.[15] It must have created somewhat of a conflict in Williams' mind. On the one hand, "Joe D" played for the enemies, the hated New York Yankees; on the other hand, DiMaggio was family. In a way, he was an extension of the Red Sox family through his relationship to brother Dom, who in turn was good friends with Williams.

In spite of the slow start that was dictated by injury, Williams quickly recovered to put together one of the greatest first-half performances in major league history. He entered the All-Star break with a .405 batting average, 16 home runs, and 62 RBIs. Not surprisingly, Williams was selected to start the All Star Game for the American League at Briggs Stadium in Detroit. With Arky Vaughan of the Pittsburgh Pirates hitting a pair of home runs for the National League, the first eight innings of the midsummer exhibition did not proceed well for the AL. The junior circuit trailed the game, 5–3, heading to the bottom of the ninth, in part because Williams had struck out with runners on in the bottom of the eighth, suppressing an AL rally.

With a capable pitcher like Claude Passeau of the Chicago Cubs on the mound, the National League seemed to have the game well in hand, especially when Passeau retired the first batter of the ninth, Frankie Hayes, on a pop-up. With one out, Cleveland Indians third baseman Ken Keltner provided a sliver of hope by legging out an infield hit. Joe Gordon followed with a single, giving the AL more realistic reasons for optimism. Passeau then pitched very carefully to Washington Senators shortstop Cecil Travis, one of the league's best hitters over the first half, and ended up walking him to load the bases.

The heart of the American League's order—Joe DiMaggio and Williams—was scheduled to bat next. DiMaggio hit a ground ball to shortstop, a potential game-ending double-play ball. The National League infield succeeded in picking up the force out at second base, but Billy Herman's throw to first base ran wide, pulling first baseman Frank McCormack off the bag. The failed double play enabled a run to score and allowed the fleet-footed DiMaggio to reach first. With runners at first and third and two outs, Williams stepped into the spotlight at Briggs Stadium.

Recent history favored Passeau, who had retired Williams on a called third strike to end what had seemed like a promising rally in the eighth. After a discussion with his infielders, Passeau hoped to repeat the feat against Williams in the ninth. Employing his trademark slider, Passeau jumped ahead of Williams, who swung late at a low pitch and fouled it off. Passeau then missed with his next two pitches, both finishing wide of the outside corner. Realizing that he had swung just a bit behind Passeau's hard slider on the first pitch, Williams told himself to quicken his bat against the next pitch, which he also anticipated to be a slider. Williams sped up his wrists appropriately, sending Passeau's pitch far toward right field; the monumental drive eventually landed in the third deck of the right-field stands. Representing one of the most memorable moments in All Star Game history, Williams' dramatic three-run shot gave the American League a 7–5 win.

Although the game was merely an exhibition and would have no impact on the pennant race in either league, the dramatic finish affected all of the winning participants. Williams reacted with an unusual show of emotion, clapping his hands, laughing and leaping as he rounded the bases, and generally prancing his way toward home, where he accepted a congratulatory handshake from DiMaggio. (Williams later referred to the home run as the most thrilling of his career.) Similarly, his American League teammates reacted as if their team had just concluded a World Series championship. Most of the players from the home dugout charged out onto the field to greet their midsummer hero. The onrushing force included Indians ace Bob Feller, who had started the game but had long since departed and was now dressed in street clothes. Tigers manager Del Baker, the skipper of the American League squad, came out onto the familiar field at Briggs Stadium and expressed his jubilation to the extreme, kissing Williams.[16] The Red Sox hierarchy, represented by general manager Eddie Collins and owner Tom Yawkey, also made its way onto the field, entering from the box seats at Briggs Stadium. Both Collins and Yawkey congratulated their young Red Sox prodigy, who had made himself a household name in front of a sellout crowd and a nationwide radio audience.

Not satisfied with earning MVP honors in the All Star Game, Williams continued his unusual level of hitting as the regular season resumed. Williams' second-half performance only solidified his status as a newfound summer celebrity. While most baseball experts figured his .400 batting average would tail off significantly after the All-Star break, it didn't. Williams maintained an average close to or above .400 throughout July, August, and September, putting him in position to make more pastime history.

Ted entered the final day of the regular season with a batting average of .3995. Under baseball's rules, that figure would be rounded up to an even .400. So if Williams didn't play on the final day at Philadelphia's Shibe Park against the A's—in either of the two games that comprised Boston's season-ending doubleheader—he would become the first .400 hitter since Bill Terry of the New York Giants in 1930. Some members of the media speculated that Williams might take himself out of the lineup the final day so as to preserve the milestone mark.

Shortly after arriving at the ballpark that day, Sox manager Joe Cronin asked Ted whether he wanted to sit out the doubleheader. "Sit out?" Ted thought to himself.[17] That was something he had never considered. He had spent most of the previous night nervously walking the streets of Philadelphia with his friend

Johnny Orlando, the Red Sox clubhouse attendant, thinking about how he would do in the doubleheader, whether he would be able to maintain his .400 average. But sit out? According to Ted, that possibility had never even crossed his mind.[18] He didn't want to reach .400 the cowardly way; he only wanted .400 if he could play the games as scheduled.

Williams also didn't like the idea of having to round his average upward to reach .400. "I'll play," Williams said without hesitation. "Hitting .3995 ain't hitting .400. If I'm going to be a .400 hitter, I want more than my toenails on the line."[19] (Williams may have been right not just in philosophy, but in practicality. According to Williams expert Bill Nowlin, there were some members of the press who felt that an average of .3995 should not have been rounded up to .400. If Williams had sat out the final two games, it is possible that his final average might have been listed at .399, and not .400.)

Playing on an overcast day in Philadelphia, Williams took his first at-bat of the afternoon against the A's. The Philadelphia crowd cheered him vehemently, admiring the courage that he was showing in playing the games. As Williams stepped into the batter's box to face pitcher Dick Fowler, he heard some cautionary but polite words from A's catcher Frankie Hayes. "I wish you all the luck in the world, Ted. But Mr. Mack told us he'd run us all out of baseball if we let up on you. You're going to have to earn it."[20] Expecting nothing less, Ted promptly singled to lift his average cleanly above .400.

The next time, Williams fared even better, depositing a 440-foot home run over the right-field wall. For his third at-bat, Connie Mack pulled Fowler and replaced him with left-hander Porter Vaughn, who ran the count to 3-and-2. Vaughn then threw a curveball toward the outside corner, but neither the angle nor the pitch bothered Williams, who lined a single into the outfield. He then picked up another single in his next at-bat, also against Vaughn. At 4-for-4, Ted was now well above the .400 mark. In his fifth at-bat, Williams reached on an error, which actually reduced his batting average slightly, but not nearly enough to put the magic mark in peril.

A number of fans and media predicted that Williams would not play the second game of the doubleheader, what with his average solidly above .400. Not so. With no thought given to sitting out the nightcap, Williams started the next game with yet another hit, a single. In his second at-bat, he delivered a ground-rule double that rather symbolically applied some damage to the ballpark. Williams' drive banged against a loudspeaker horn located on top of the right-field wall, leaving a discernible dent on the Shibe Park fixture.[21] With the latest piece of offensive destruction in the books, Williams was now 6-for-7 on the day. From there he would "slump" a little, enduring a hitless appearance in his final turn at-bat. Yet, he had already given himself a sufficiently large cushion in maintaining the milestone. Rather than having to rely on the mathematicians to generously round his average up to .400, Williams had succeeded in taking on the more legitimate path to glory, a much harder path. He had finished the season at .406, making his .400 season far more indelible than if he had taken the safe way and simply sat out the final two games.

A closer examination of Williams' statistics in 1941 provided some intriguing revelations. His on-base percentage reached a staggering level, a mark of .553—uncharted territory for most batters. Although he hit for an incredibly high average and drew 147 walks, he didn't sacrifice power, hitting 37 home runs. And while he continued to hit with power, he almost never failed to make contact, striking out only 27 times.

Williams' ability to hit .400 ranked as even more remarkable considering the lack of infield hits he amassed that season while playing with an injured leg. "To tell you the truth, I chipped a bone in my ankle in 1941, and it was taped through most of the season," Williams told sportswriter Ed Linn. "They forget that now. I don't think I had many leg hits at all that year, because I couldn't run too well."[22]

So how did Williams manage to break the .400 barrier? He took full advantage of his home field. Williams hit .428 in games at Fenway Park, a ballpark known for the favorable conditions that it supplied hitters. With its small amount of foul territory and a pleasing batter's eye screen provided by the center-field background, Williams found Fenway to his liking. He did well against the strong pitching of the rival Yankees at Fenway, hitting .457 in home games against New York. Yet, he did even better in games at New York (hitting .485 in the Bronx), helping him hit .471 overall against the Yankees' standout staff that summer.

No matter how one divided or categorized the statistics, they provided profitable bottom line results for Williams and the Red Sox. Yet the question remained; how did Williams do it? After all, the notion of a .400 hitter has become a thing of the past since Williams' performance, with the mark never having been reached in the years since 1941. What was it about Williams' abilities and approach made him capable of reaching one of the most elusive batting milestones in recent baseball history? Writers and broadcasters alike tried to offer reasons for Williams' unmatched hitting ability. In an article that appeared during the summer of 1941, *Life* magazine provided a paragraph of sound reasoning, accompanied by a series of still black-and-white photographs (pictures taken at high speeds) that showed a barechested Williams engaged in the hitting process, from the beginning of the swing to the ending follow-through. "Williams is a great hitter for three reasons: eyes, wrists, and forearms," claimed the article in *Life*. "He has what ballplayers call 'camera eyes,' which allow him to focus on a pitched ball as it zooms down its sixty-foot path from the pitcher's hand, accurately judge its intended path across the plate, and reach for it. He even claims he can see the ball and bat meet."[23] According to one urban legend, Williams possessed such keen eyesight that he could read the label on a record as it was spinning on a 78 RPM turntable. It made for a great story, but Williams repeatedly denied that it was true.[24]

Throughout his career, Williams frequently tried to minimize the notion that his terrific eyesight carried him to greatness, if only because it detracted from what he considered the real reason behind his success at the plate. "They say the secret of my hitting is natural ability and my good eyesight," Williams told *Sports Illustrated* in a 1955 interview. "A lot of people have as good eyesight as I have and probably better, and still they're always ready to say, 'Eyesight's the reason he does it—and natural ability.' That's so easy to say and to give credit for. They never talk about the practice. Practice! Practice! Practice! Dammit, you gotta practice!"[25]

Nonetheless, Williams' keen 20/10 eyesight (sometimes listed as 20/15) did provide a scene-setting stage for one of the game's most beautiful and powerful swings, a swing that was driven by unusually strong wrists and forearms. "On and off the field he constantly wields a bat to keep the spring in his powerful wrists," *Life* explained. "And, more than most other great batters, he keeps his body out of his swing, puts all his drive into his forearms."[26]

In looking back at his remarkable 1941 season, Williams recalled achieving far better results while using the same techniques that he had always employed at the plate. "First time it ever happened in my life like that and I was just doing what I was trying to do all the time, hit the ball hard," Williams told the Hall of Fame, before suggesting that weaker pitching might have contributed to his success.

> I think that in all careers, in all outstanding performances—baseball, football, basketball—all of them go in cycles. Now DiMaggio hit in 56 games that same year, so it's possible that maybe pitching wasn't as strong [as the hitting that year], I can't say that because I'm not sure. I do know there were several guys that hit well that year, so you have to think maybe pitching was at a little lower level, I don't know. Then you go into [bad] cycles where, boy, there's about 12 [good] pitchers in the league that really blow it. They have great years and the weather's been lousy for the year, which was a detriment to the hitting, the wind was blowing in or it was rainy and windy. You might have a year or two where averages are reflected by that weather. You know, nothing's stamped in iron. . . . But in all sports, just imagine if [Joe] Louis was fighting when Muhammad Ali come up. I saw

Louis when he was a young guy, I thought absolutely nobody could
ever beat that guy, until I saw Muhammad Ali at the end and he told
you what he was going to do, and he was a great, great athlete. So
you know you got to take them in [their] eras. Ruth was playing; he
was just a step ahead of anybody in the power department. Only one
guy could challenge at that time—Jimmie Foxx. Then you go down
the line a little further and [Ty] Cobb came into the picture . . . he
was aggressive, he was fast, he was proud of what he could do. Competitive, gee, what a competitor. I don't think anybody will ever—
some of his records have been broken—but [that lifetime batting
average of] .367, I don't think it's going to be broken. I even think
it might be harder to [break] that than when he was playing.[27]

Despite reaching the .400 mark with that unmatched combination of "eyes,
wrists, and forearms," and torturing opposing pitchers throughout the season,
Williams did not seem to receive his just due, at least not from the sportswriters that covered the game. In voting announced after the season, Williams found
out that he did not win the AL's MVP Award, instead finishing second to the
Yankees' Joe DiMaggio. It was a result that stunned some observers. In exam-
ining reasons for what some perceived as a snub by the media, some pointed to
DiMaggio's fifty-six-game hitting streak and the attention that it garnered for
two months of the season. Others focused on Williams' difficult demeanor with
reporters, which might have topped the list of reasons for the order of the voting. Other critics, concerned with the final standings for each of the MVP candidates' teams, dwelled on the Red Sox futile finish, which placed them
seventeen games behind the Yankees. Still others cited a combination of the
above reasons for Williams' seemingly shortchanged finish in the MVP sweepstakes.

Although Williams and most frenzied followers of the Red Sox found cause
to differ with what they considered biased voting by the writers, such concerns
soon become unimportant given real world occurrences. On December 7, 1941,
unexpected tragedy struck the United States, not on the mainland but on one
of its outposts—the recently accessed territory of Hawaii. More specifically, it
was a brutal surprise military attack on Pearl Harbor, plotted and staged by the
Japanese, who were already involved in the global conflict of World War II. In
addition to claiming hundreds of American lives, the air attack on Pearl Harbor forced the United States to enter the war effort, a decision that would come
to affect the sport of baseball along with almost every aspect of American culture. Like many other professional ballplayers, both in the minor and major
leagues, Ted Williams would not be spared the potential calamities of war.

NOTES

1. Interview with Ted Williams, conducted by Jeff Idelson of the National Baseball Hall of Fame, 2000.

2. Ibid.

3. Correspondence with Bill Nowlin, 2003.

4. Interview with Ted Williams, conducted by Jeff Idelson of the National Baseball Hall of Fame, 2000.

5. Riley, *The Red Sox Reader*, 56.

6. Pietrusza et al., *Baseball*, 1236.

7. Williams, with Pietrusza, *Teddy Ballgame*, 37.

8. Interview with Ted Williams, conducted by Jeff Idelson of the National Baseball Hall of Fame, 2000.

9. Davis, *The Scribner Encyclopedia of American Lives*, 502.

10. Pietrusza et al., *Baseball*, 1236.

11. Richard Goldstein and Robert McG. Thomas, "Ted Williams, Red Sox Slugger and Last To Hit .400, Dies At 83," *New York Times*, July 6, 2002, A1, D4.

12. Bryant, *Shut Out*, 25.

13. Gordon Edes, "Ted Williams: A Life Remembered—The Keyboards Were Always Spelling Trouble," *Boston Globe*, July 6, 2002, online edition.

14. Dreyspool, "Ted Williams," 58.

15. Pietrusza et al., *Baseball*, 1236.

16. Williams, with Pietrusza, *Teddy Ballgame*, 46.

17. Ibid., 47.

18. Ibid., 47.

19. Greene, "Ted Williams' Ten Greatest Days," 26.

20. Ibid.

21. Riley, *The Red Sox Reader*, 57.

22. Linn, "Growing Up With Ted," 56.

23. "Williams of the Red Sox Is Best Hitter," *Life*, September 1, 1941, 43.

24. Shaughnessy, "The Kid," 76.

25. Dreyspool, "Ted Williams," 29.

26. "Williams of the Red Sox Is Best Hitter," 43–44.

27. Interview with Ted Williams, conducted by Jeff Idelson of the National Baseball Hall of Fame, 2000.

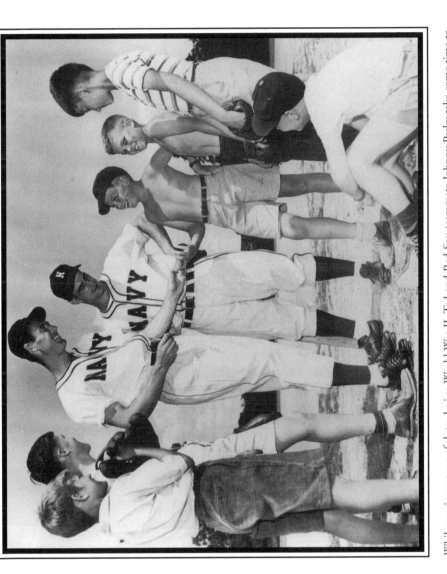

While serving a tour of duty during World War II, Ted and Red Sox teammate Johnny Pesky take some time to talk baseball with a group of younger players. *National Baseball Hall of Fame Library, Cooperstown, N.Y.*

4

WAR FIRST, BASEBALL A DISTANT SECOND

In the weeks and months after Pearl Harbor, a number of major league players enlisted in the U.S. military. The list of servicemen included star players, such as Bob Feller of the Cleveland Indians and Hank Greenberg of the Detroit Tigers. With such superstars not excluded from wartime service, some writers began to speculate about the possibility of Ted Williams entering the armed services. Williams had previously been classified as 3-A, which was a military deferment that prevented him from being drafted. He had been granted such status because of his parents' divorce in 1939, coupled with his brother's inability to provide financial assistance. As a result, Ted alone represented the sole monetary support for his mother.[1]

Yet, Ted's military status suddenly changed in 1942, when he received official word that he had been reclassified as 1-A, making him eligible for the military draft. Williams felt the decision was wrong and unfair, motivating him to file an appeal, based on his claim that his mother be considered his dependent. The appeal went to a presidential board, which determined that Williams should once again be classified as 3-A. Once again, he was exempt from the draft.[2]

With America now at war, some fans wondered about the fairness of Williams' exemption and openly booed him at the ballpark, or wrote letters of complaint to him and the Red Sox. Some members of the media became skeptical, as well. To the writers, it didn't matter that Williams' parents were divorced; they felt Williams was receiving preferential treatment because of his celebrity status as a ballplayer. One Boston newspaper decided to investigate the matter further by sending a private detective to Williams' home in San Diego. Another local newspaper assigned reporters to conduct "man on the street" interviews, soliciting opinions on whether Williams should be considered non-patriotic for his efforts to exclude himself from military service. Williams even lost one of his endorsement opportunities, as the Quaker Oats company decided to cancel its $4,000 contract with its star client.[3]

Sensitive to such slights, Williams considered the criticism heavily. Although he felt he was legitimately categorized as 3-A and believed himself to be right in the matter, his pride was affected by some of the barbs he received. With public pressure growing, Williams decided to change his original decision. In May of 1942, Williams visited the naval recruiting station located on Causeway Street and officially enrolled himself in the military effort. Williams signed up for aviation training in the Navy air corps and received a second lieutenant's commission. Yet, Williams would not have to report for duty until the end of the 1942 season. That way, he would be able to earn another full season's salary with the Red Sox, giving him additional money that he would pass off to his mother.[4]

Perhaps distracted by his impending military involvement and his mother's precarious financial condition, Williams saw his batting average fall off to .356. For most players, such a season would have marked the highlight of a career; for Ted, it was a fifty-point dropoff from his hallmark season of 1941. Such was the price for setting such a high standard of excellence with a bat in his hand.

After officially reporting for naval duty in November, Williams attended ground school training in Amherst, Massachusetts. Williams took part in the civilian pilot training program, which involved a great deal of classroom study, including course work in aerodynamics and navigation, among other pursuits. The program's trainees also included several other major league players. Williams' cadet class featured Red Sox teammates Bobby Doerr and Johnny Pesky and opposing players Joe Coleman and Johnny Sain.[5]

Yet, Williams did not receive preferential treatment. He had to work hard both in the classroom and in the gym, putting in long hours of exercise and physical training. Driven by his instructors throughout his training, Williams ended up suffering a hernia, which resulted in a two-month stay at Chelsea Naval Hospital.[6]

Although Williams suffered physical setbacks, he displayed excellent mental aptitude for the rigorous course work mandated by the naval training. His classroom efforts were especially impressive considering that he had not attended a college or university, his formal schooling having come to an end with his graduation from high school. After his stay at Amherst, Ted moved onto Chapel Hill, North Carolina, where he underwent rigorous preflight training. Given the high standard of conditioning demanded by the Navy, Williams had to push his body to extreme limits; one of the typical naval exercises required that he stay afloat in water for up to an hour.[7]

Williams also found a small amount of spare time to play some military baseball on weekends, as part of the Navy's team at Chapel Hill Preflight School. Williams' Chapel Hill teammates included Johnny Pesky, the Red Sox starting shortstop, and several other major league veterans, including Harry Craft, Buddy Hassett, and Johnny Sain.[8]

From North Carolina, Williams reported to a naval air station in Indiana, where he had to put 100 hours of actual flight time as part of basic flight training. After a term in Indiana, Williams made two more stopovers in Florida—one in Pensacola and another in Jacksonville—as part of the military's advanced training process.[9] During his time in Florida, Williams displayed outstanding technique as a pilot and decided to apply for instructor's school as a way of continuing to sharpen his skills for future combat. Williams became a fine instructor, teaching young pilots in various squadrons to fly. His skill as a gunnery pilot was particularly impressive to those who watched him. While in Jacksonville, Williams set a number of gunnery records that remain unsurpassed.[10]

By now, Williams had received most of the operational training that he needed to become a fighter pilot and actually take part in wartime missions. He then moved on to San Francisco, with instructions to eventually report to Hawaii, which would be the last stop on his training tour.[11]

Then came the news of August 15, when Williams, the military, and the rest of the American public learned about the declaration of V-J (Victory in Japan) Day. With the surrender of the Japanese, United States participation in World War II had come to an end. Despite all of the training that he had received, Ted would not see live combat during the Second World War. With the war over, he expected an immediate return to his native San Diego, but was told he would still have to remain on call for further duty. In the military, orders were orders, and they would have to be followed to the letter, even with American troops withdrawing from Europe and Japan.

After finishing out his military stint in Hawaii, Ted finally received permission to return home.[12] On January 12, 1946, he officially earned his discharge from the military, capping off a three-year stint of service in World War II. Although Williams had been fortunate enough to escape actual combat abroad, he had missed three full seasons of what were generally considered prime years of his athletic career. Unlike most other professions, which can be performed capably in one's thirties, forties, or even later years, the prime of a baseball player's career usually falls in his mid-to-late twenties. Three of those seasons had been lost to Ted—and could never be gained back. Nonetheless, Williams refused to dwell on what might have been and remained determined to continue the career that he had chosen since he was a child.

NOTES

1. Williams, with Pietrusza, *Teddy Ballgame*, 53.

2. Ibid.

3. Ibid.

4. David Pietrusza, lecture at the National Baseball Hall of Fame in Cooperstown, NY, June 6, 2003.

5. Williams, with Pietrusza, *Teddy Ballgame*, 54.

6. Ibid.

7. Bill Nowlin and Jim Prime, *Ted Williams: The Pursuit of Perfection* (Champaign, IL: Sports Publishing, 2002), 80.

8. Williams, with Pietrusza, *Teddy Ballgame*, 57.

9. Correspondence with Bill Nowlin, 2003.

10. Ibid.

11. Williams, with Pietrusza, *Teddy Ballgame*, 54.

12. Ibid., and correspondence with Bill Nowlin, 2003.

5

BACK TO BASEBALL

The wartime years changed Williams in more ways than one. In addition to gaining extensive aviation experience and an increased level of maturity, Williams also married for the first time. On May 4, 1944, Williams wed Doris Soule, whom he had first met six years earlier while playing minor league ball in Minnesota.

While Ted juggled his personal life, his fortunes in the baseball world turned better at the end of the war. By 1946, the Red Sox had assembled a good supporting cast behind Williams; the nucleus included hard-hitting Rudy York at first base, good friend and fellow San Diego Padres alumnus Bobby Doerr at second base, military compatriot Johnny Pesky at shortstop, and the subtly-skilled Dom DiMaggio in center field. Prior to and during the war, the Red Sox had suffered through lean years. They had a few star players, like Williams and Doerr, but lacked All-Star players at other positions, the requisite depth needed to contend, and perhaps most importantly, the kind of quality pitching that is associated with pennant-winning teams. By now, most of those shortcomings had been overcome. Coinciding with the end of the war, the Red Sox found themselves with sufficient talent to emerge as a contending team in the American League pennant race.

Both Williams and the Red Sox enjoyed a solid first half of the 1946 season. Hitting a robust .347 with 23 home runs, Williams played well enough to earn a starting berth in the All Star Game, scheduled for July 9, marking his first appearance in the Midsummer Classic since 1942. Williams, who had already cemented his All Star Game reputation with a game-winning home run against Claude Passeau, only added to that reputation in July of 1946. Appropriately

Williams displays the balance that helped make him arguably the game's greatest hitter. Notice how the bat actually bends as Williams nears the end of his swing. *National Baseball Hall of Fame Library, Cooperstown, N.Y.*

enough, the game took place at Fenway Park, Ted's home field. In his first at-bat of the game, Williams once again faced Passeau, marking a five-year reunion of sorts between the two All-Stars. Williams worked the count against Passeau to 3-and-2, before drawing a walk and eventually coming home to score on a home run by the Yankees Charlie "King Kong" Keller.

In the fourth inning, Williams hit a home run of his own, connecting against Kirby Higbe and reaching the right-center-field bleachers at Fenway. Williams followed that blast with another hit, this time an RBI single against Ewell "The Whip" Blackwell in the fifth inning. He added another single two innings later, once again reaching base against Blackwell to ignite a 2-run rally.

Williams wasn't done. Having already blasted one home run in the All Star Game, Williams would supply an even more memorable moment later in the game. Facing Truett "Rip" Sewell of the Pittsburgh Pirates, a pitcher who had added the famed "eephus" or "blooper" pitch to his repertoire earlier that season, Williams tried to accomplish what few felt could be done—hit a home run against the high-arcing pitch. (In fact, no one had homered against Sewell's eephus pitch that season; Stan Musial had been the most successful, managing a triple against the eephus.) A pregame conversation that Williams had enjoyed with a Hall of Fame catcher would provide him with some much-needed insight on Sewell's trick pitch.

"Bill Dickey and I were sitting on the bench," Williams recalled in an interview with the Hall of Fame. "[Sewell] looked in and he saw Bill Dickey and he saw me there. I don't know what he heard or what he suspected, but he said to me, 'You're going to get it.' That's all he said, 'You're going to get it.' Of course, we knew what he was talking about because we had been talking about the eephus pitch. The ball just getting over the plate for a called strike was a pretty good [accomplishment], but he could do it. I told Bill, 'Nobody can hit a homer off that pitch.' Bill Dickey said to me, 'You can.'"[1] Because Sewell's pitch reached an arc of twenty to twenty-five feet above the ground, Dickey suggested that Williams "run up" in the batter's box, taking one or two steps forward as the pitch was being delivered, as if he were facing a slow-pitch softball pitcher.

With two runners on base, Williams anticipated the first pitch from Sewell. Surely enough, it was the blooper, or eephus pitch. Williams grinned widely as he looked the pitch over, then took a hard swing and lined it foul. Sewell followed up the eephus by throwing a standard fastball, which either Williams didn't anticipate or purposely let slip by him. Either way, the pitch registered another strike, putting the count at 0-and-2.

Severely down in the count, Williams anticipated the eephus pitch. "He could get that damn pitch over," Williams recalled, "and he didn't throw it harder than a softball, but he could get [it] called a strike. I bet there's no pitcher in the big leagues that could throw that type of pitch and get it over the plate before he walked."[2] After Sewell released the ball and it began its downward descent, Williams took two steps towards the pitcher's mound, as Dickey had recommended. With his front foot actually out of the batter's box, Williams made contact with the pitch. "And when I got the eephus pitch," Williams said, "I swung as hard as I could. . . ."[3]

Supplying all of the power himself while aided slightly by an outgoing breeze, Williams lifted the eephus pitch beyond the outfield wall and into the right-field bullpen—about 380 feet away from home plate—for a remarkable home run. As famed writer John Updike penned in the *New Yorker*, "It was like hitting a balloon out of the park."[4] The unlikely home run capped off a game that saw Williams finish with 2 four-baggers, 2 singles, a walk, and 5 single-game All-Star records: most home runs (2), most hits (4), most runs scored (4), most RBIs (5), and most total bases (10). With Williams doing much of the damage, the American League won the game handily, 12–0.

The 1946 season provided more legendary fodder for the Williams resume. On July 14, Williams and the Red Sox faced the Indians, led by their player-manager Lou Boudreau. Cleveland's All-Star shortstop collected four doubles and a home run in the first game of a doubleheader. Yet, it was not Boudreau who emerged as the headline-maker in the lidlifter. That honor belonged to Williams, who overshadowed Boudreau by hitting three home runs and pulling a double down the right-field line, while driving in eight runs to lead the Sox to an 11–10 win.

In the second game of the doubleheader, Boudreau made some news of his own, not as a player, but from a managerial standpoint. He decided to use an unusual shift against Williams. In situations where the Red Sox had no one on base, Boudreau placed six defenders to the right of second base (the third baseman, shortstop, second baseman, first baseman, center fielder and right fielder) and left only one to the left of second base (the left fielder). Only the catcher and pitcher played their normal positions; they would have to do so, as dictated by baseball's official playing rules.

As part of the shift, Indians third baseman Ken Keltner moved from his usual position to a spot located just to the right of the second base. Boudreau moved himself from his accustomed position even further to the right side of the second base bag, placing him in a location previously held by the second baseman. The Indians' regular second baseman, Dutch Meyer, moved in behind Boudreau, playing what amounted to a shallow right field.

Boudreau's strategic defense against Williams became known as the "Williams

Shift" or the "Boudreau Shift," depending on whether your perspective favored Boston or Cleveland. Although Boudreau's maneuver garnered the attention of the media, the concept of a shift had actually been employed many years earlier. On occasion, American League teams had repositioned their fielders against Babe Ruth, who also tended to pull the ball.[5] Furthermore, an unusual shift against Williams had actually originated in 1941, when manager Roger Peckinpaugh of the Cleveland Indians decided to use it.[6] The original shift against Williams didn't attract much notice from the media, since Peckinpaugh abandoned it almost as quickly as he devised it.

Surprised but not flustered by Boudreau's strategy against him, Williams refused to give in to the shift. "I was just trying to prepare myself to be ready to hit," Williams said of the shift that remained in use (though not all of the time) until being mostly bypassed during the 1959 and 1960 seasons.[7] "Hit it hard, not hit it to the left or not hit it over here. Hit the ball hard. That's all I really ever thought about, just hit the ball hard."[8] Williams opted not to try to punch singles to left field or lay down bunts down the third-base line, as a way of picking up cheap singles against the shift. As a matter of philosophy, he did not want to unnecessarily alter his swing, which he considered a dangerous temptation, one that could ruin his finely tuned approach at the plate. He also believed it was more important to try to hit with power; he felt that extra-base hits and home runs would help the team more than a meager bunt or a trickling grounder down the third base line. Of course, there did occur a few exceptions to Williams' philosophy, times when he decided to hit to left field against the shift. One of those exceptions would come in a crucial situation late that season, as the Red Sox fought for the lead in the American League.

In August of 1946, Red Sox fans showed their growing appreciation for Williams and the Red Sox in a special day at Fenway Park. A group of fans from Gardner, Massachusetts, a town noted for its furniture industry, descended on downtown Boston. They brought with them several pieces of furniture and some equipment, some of which could be classified as unusual. The furniture included a massive wooden chair—big enough to seat four or five men or a single giant—which Williams sat on for photographers before it was placed on a truck and returned to Gardner.[9] The equipment included a giant-sized bat, one that required two to three people just to lift it. As a gift, the fans from Gardner presented the unique bat to Williams,[10] who donated it to the National Baseball Hall of Fame and Museum, where it remains on display to this day.

While Williams found temporary amusement and distraction from his newly encountered friends in Gardner, he also experienced a new challenge on the field:

participating in a pennant race. As much individual success as he had experienced since breaking into the big leagues in 1939, meaningful team accomplishments had eluded the Red Sox. That began to change in August and September of 1946, when the Red Sox opened up a lead in the American League race. By early September, the Red Sox were closing in on what they hoped would be a pennant celebration.

On September 13, the Red Sox and Indians found themselves in a scoreless tie. Williams saw an opportunity to break the deadlock by intentionally trying to hit the ball to left field, against his natural tendency. So Williams defied the Boudreau Shift and pounded the ball toward left field. By the time the Indians' outfield had retrieved the ball and returned it to the infield, Williams had circled the bases. He had succeeded in hitting an inside-the-park home run to left field (the only such home run of his career). The strange, opposite field homer supplied the only run of the game, giving Boston a critical victory that clinched the American League pennant for the Red Sox.

For Williams, it marked the first—and only—pennant celebration of his major league career. For the Red Sox, it was their first American League championship since 1918, the last year in which they owned a star pitcher-outfielder named Babe Ruth. By the end of the 1946 season, the Red Sox had clearly distanced themselves from the rest of the American League pack, finishing twelve games ahead of the second-place Tigers and earning a berth in the World Series against the National League titlists. Several Red Sox stood out in fulfilling the role of pennant-winners. Second-year starter Dave "Boo" Ferriss won twenty-five games, an impressive follow-up to his twenty-one-win campaign as a rookie. Shortstop Johnny Pesky batted .335, accumulating over 200 hits for the second season in a row. Dom DiMaggio batted .316 and precisely patrolled center field. Second baseman Bobby Doerr supplied an appetizing combination of middle infield power and skilled glove work.

And then there was Williams, who nearly won the Triple Crown. In spite of the long absence from competitive baseball, Williams had returned to the major leagues by hitting .342, with 38 home runs and 123 RBIs in 1946. Given such gaudy numbers, many fans expected Williams to continue his success in the postseason. Yet, such expectations gave way to the game's general unpredictability. Just prior to the Series, on October 1, the Red Sox played the first exhibition game of a series against a team of American League All-Stars while the St. Louis Cardinals and Brooklyn Dodgers settled the National League pennant with a three-game play-off. Williams was hit on the elbow with a pitch thrown by Mickey Haefner. The incident, which left Williams in pain and his elbow tender for several days, may have had a profound effect on the way that Williams would be remembered for his postseason performance. With the elbow badly swollen by the errant pitch, Williams gritted with pain throughout the Series. The discomfort would not leave his arm until after the Series had concluded.

Another factor may have affected Williams as well. Just prior to the Series, a pair of major trade rumors made their way through the baseball world. According to one rumor, the Red Sox would trade Williams to the Detroit Tigers after the Series. Neither the timing of the speculation or the rumor itself made much sense, but the scuttlebutt succeeded in disturbing Williams.[11] According to another rumor, the Red Sox had already completed a blockbuster trade that would send Williams to the New York Yankees in a one-for-one swap involving Joe DiMaggio. "I guess I'll miss Boston," a gullible Williams would say after Game One, apparently believing the Yankee rumor to be true. "I know my way around there. What'll I do in New York on off days?"[12]

Wild trade rumors and injuries aside, the Red Sox played the role of considerable favorites as they faced the St. Louis Cardinals in the World Series. Still, the Cardinals featured a core of standout players, including the deft double-play combination of future Hall-of-Famer Red Schoendienst and slick-fielding shortstop Marty Marion, and two Hall of Fame outfield bookends, Stan Musial (the National League's MVP) and Enos "Country" Slaughter. That quartet of players, along with center fielder Terry Moore, formed the cornerstone of one of the best defensive alignments in all of baseball.

During the Series, Cardinals manager Eddie Dyer decided to employ a shift of his defensive players against Williams, similar to the one that Lou Boudreau had introduced during the regular season. Under the Dyer shift, third baseman Whitey Kurowski relocated all the way to the right side of the second-base bag, while Marty Marion moved only slightly to the right of his normal position at shortstop. With the third baseman, second baseman, and first baseman all on the right side of the diamond, Williams managed only a harmless single in the first game, but barely missed hitting a home run when he drove a fly ball off the screen in right field, foul by just a few inches. In spite of Williams' lack of impact on the game, the Red Sox still won, 3–2. Down to their last strike, the Sox rallied for a run in the ninth to tie, then won the game when Rudy York clubbed a tenth inning pitch into the left-field bleachers. The Red Sox then dropped Game 2, losing 3–0 to Harry "The Cat" Brecheen, who spun a four-hitter. Williams failed to pick up a hit in the second game, unable to even push the ball past the shifted infield against Brecheen.

After Williams struggled against Cardinals pitching in the first two games, he decided to do something highly uncharacteristic in Game 3. With one out in the third inning and Dyer still tilting his fielders to the right, Ted tried to bunt against the shift, a strategy that he had purposely avoided during the season.

Born of frustration—and perhaps even desperation—Williams' attempt at bunting symbolized his struggles swinging the bat during the Series.

Williams' strategy proved fruitful, at least in the short term. With the left side of the Cardinals' infield wide open, Williams managed to push the ball to the right of the third-base bag. The ball made its way to the outfield, allowing Williams to reach first base with ease. Although Rudy York crushed a key 3-run home run in the first inning and the Red Sox went on to win the game behind Dave Ferriss' shutout pitching—their first World Series win at Fenway since 1918—much of the post-game media attention centered on Williams' decision to bunt. Some writers criticized Williams for his choice, saying that he had allowed the Cardinals' defensive shift to alter his proven method of hitting. One newspaper featured a headline that read "WILLIAMS BUNTS,"[13] rather than simply highlighting the fact that the Red Sox had won a critical game in the Series. A 4–0 victory apparently didn't make for the kind of good copy that could be produced by an unorthodox piece of strategy by Ted Williams.

Taking a two-games-to-one lead in the Series, the Red Sox seemed primed to put away the Cardinals, especially if Williams started to hit. Neither development occurred in Game 4, as the Red Sox fell, 12–3. The Cardinals combined for twenty hits against Red Sox pitchers, marking their worst performance of the Series.

Still, the Red Sox showed resiliency in Game Five. Williams continued to flail at the plate, but journeyman outfielder Leon Culberson homered and right-hander Joe Dobson pitched the Sox to victory. The 6–3 win put Boston one game away from its first World Championship since 1918.

As he did in Game 2, Harry Brecheen mastered Red Sox hitters in the sixth game. A 4–1 decision in favor of the Cardinals evened the Series at three games apiece, setting the scene for an ultimate Game 7 at Sportsman's Park.

The Red Sox staked themselves to an early lead in the seventh game, scoring a single run in the top of the first against Murry Dickson. They almost scored a second, but St. Louis' gifted center fielder, Terry Moore, frustrated Williams by robbing him of an extra-base hit and an RBI. In the fourth inning, Williams again delivered a long drive, only to have it run down by another fleet Cardinals outfielder, Harry "The Hat" Walker. Williams' two long outs, certainly no fault of his own, became even more noteworthy when the Cardinals scored two runs against Ferriss in the fifth to take the lead.

Playing on the road and down by two runs, the Sox continued to play hard. Their offense, continuing to grind but unable to score since the first, finally re-emerged in the top of the eighth, when Dom DiMaggio sounded a clutch double, scoring two runs. Unfortunately, DiMaggio turned his ankle while rounding first base and had to leave the game. Yet, he had succeeded in tying the score at 3–3, placing the Red Sox in a position to directly determine their fates in the final two innings.

Leading off the bottom of the eighth, the Cardinals hustling star, Enos Slaughter, delivered a single, but then watched Whitey Kurowski and catcher Del Rice come up empty. With two outs and Slaughter still at first, Harry Walker stepped to the plate. Eddie Dyer ordered the hit-and-run, a play that Walker handled capably. As Slaughter broke from first, Walker slapped a sinking liner into left center field. Backup outfielder Leon Culberson, a rag-armed center fielder who had replaced the injured DiMaggio, fielded the ball and threw weakly to Johnny Pesky, the Red Sox shortstop and cutoff man who was positioned in short left center field. As the Red Sox defenders worked the ball inward, Slaughter raced for third and rounded the bag. Third base coach Mike Gonzalez either gave him a stop sign or no sign (reports vary on this matter), but Slaughter continued his sprint toward home plate.

According to baseball legend, Pesky hesitated by fully turning to his left and then throwing, surprised that Slaughter had decided to make a break for home plate. In reality, Pesky didn't hesitate for anything more than the slightest of moments; Culberson had slowed the relay by lobbing the ball to Pesky, who in turn made a below-average throw to the plate, with the ball running up the third-base line. Slaughter scored on Walker's double, completing his famed "Mad Dash" and giving the Cardinals the decisive run in the Series.

The Red Sox lost that final game, 4–3, a heartbreaking loss given how far the Sox had come in 1946. Williams' struggles—he ended up batting .200 in the Series—didn't help Boston's cause; a more productive Williams might have meant the difference between winning and losing the Series. Immediately after the Series' conclusion, Williams sat silently in the Red Sox clubhouse. Later on, Williams displayed the emotions of a proud professional athlete who despised the disappointment and the feelings of guilt that came with losing. He cried in his train compartment, a reaction that he intended to keep private. Williams, however, failed to draw the blinds on the compartment windows, so others saw him in the midst of this unusual display.

In later years, Williams searched for answers to his World Series failure. At one point, he talked about the wind in the games at Fenway Park and how the inward gusts made it more difficult to hit,[14] but that explanation didn't satisfy him entirely. "Here we are talking about the only Series I got in," Williams told the Hall of Fame with some sense of regret. "And I did poorly, and I don't know why today. I don't know why. I got a little excuse in my own mind, but I've never mentioned it as an excuse."[15] Williams didn't expound further, but he may have been referring to the incident in which he had been hit in the elbow by a pitched ball. Or perhaps he was referencing the wild trade rumor that had him moving on to the Tigers after the World Series.

In a team sport, even lofty individual accomplishments, like the ones that Williams had achieved during the American League's regular season, fail to console the greatest of athletes. Still, Williams deserved credit for a sensational season, which seemed all the more remarkable given his three-year absence from the sport. And his performance did help the Red Sox win the American League pennant, an achievement sometimes overshadowed by World Series shortcomings. "Oh, certainly, there's a lot of satisfaction," Williams explained to the Hall of Fame. "It's not the ultimate joy, say of winning the World Series, but it's certainly two-thirds of the act."[16]

That "two-thirds of the act" would bring Williams some much-deserved acclaim. On November 15, 1946, Williams earned his due for his regular season performance when the Baseball Writers' Association of America announced the results of its Most Valuable Player election. Five years earlier, Williams had won the Triple Crown, but had lost the MVP vote to Joe DiMaggio of the Yankees. This time, Williams ran second to no one in the American League balloting. He outpolled Tigers ace Hal Newhouser, a two-time winner of the award who placed second in the voting.

Not satisfied with his MVP efforts in 1946, Williams continued to build his budding legend the following season. In 1947, Williams won the Triple Crown again, as the Red Sox fell to third place in the American League. Williams' second Triple Crown made him the only left-hander hitter to win the distinction twice during his career. In an intriguing twist, only Williams' old minor league mentor, Rogers Hornsby, had previously succeeded in winning two Triple Crowns, albeit as a right-handed hitter.

Unfortunately, Williams' second Triple Crown did relatively little to impress the voters entrusted with the handling of the American League's MVP Award. The Red Sox also-ran status in the AL clearly hurt Williams in the balloting. On November 27, 1947, Joe DiMaggio edged Williams to capture his third MVP Award. DiMaggio won the award even though Williams led the league in batting average, home runs, and RBIs. While his numbers lapped those of DiMaggio, they did little to convince the majority of writers voting for the MVP. Williams received a total of only three first-place votes (out of a possible twenty-four), leaving him narrowly behind DiMaggio in the MVP sweepstakes.

The lack of first-place support surprised some fans, but the lack of support further down the ballot showed evidence of a near travesty. According to baseball legend—and Williams' own belief—one Boston writer had failed to include Williams on his ballot. It was believed to be Mel Webb, but like all baseball myths, the common belief did not match historical reality. Webb actually didn't have a vote that year; it was a writer from the Midwest who left Williams completely off his ballot. Still, the identity of the writer didn't matter as much as the fact that *any* writer could have seen fit to ignore Williams. The snub was inexcusable, considering Williams' season. While an argument could be made that Williams didn't deserve the MVP, no reasonable discussion could have supported the decision to completely leave him off a top ten list of American League contributors. It was not a proud moment in the history of the MVP voting of the Baseball Writers' Association of America.

The start of the 1948 calendar year brought a major change to Williams' life. On January 27, Barbara Joyce Williams was born, the first child to Ted and Doris Williams, his first wife. Much to the chagrin of the Boston press, Williams was nowhere near the hospital when his daughter was born. He was in Florida on one of his usual winter fishing expeditions. Williams' absence, however, was somewhat understandable. Barbara Joyce had been born prematurely, several weeks before the expected date. Still, the Boston writers offered Williams little slack as they condemned him as being something other than a "family man." When the reporters eventually learned of Williams' divorce, which would occur six years later, they likely felt even more justified in the way they had labeled the Red Sox star.

The 1948 season also brought major change to the Red Sox landscape. Joe Cronin moved from the dugout to the front office, replacing the retiring Eddie Collins as Boston's general manager. Former Yankee manager Joe McCarthy, who had overseen New York's dynasty in the late 1930s and had also guided the Chicago Cubs to the pennant, became the Red Sox manager. While with the Yankees, McCarthy had carved a reputation as a taskmaster and strict disciplinarian, enforcing rigid rules on all of his players. For example, he had required his Yankees to wear ties and suits. Boston writers, expecting the worst, wondered how McCarthy's disciplined regimentation would sit with Red Sox players, in particular Williams, who didn't like to wear suits and refused to wear ties. Instead, Ted preferred to wear colorful sports shirts.

To the surprise of many observers, the controversy never developed. As many of the Red Sox players gathered in the team's dining room, McCarthy made his first dinnertime appearance. Everyone, including the writers, noticed that "Marse Joe" was wearing a loud sports shirt with an open neck—and no tie. Displaying an impressive willingness to adapt, McCarthy had immediately relaxed his rules with the Red Sox. McCarthy's decision appeared to be inspired almost entirely by Williams' presence in a Boston uniform. "Anyone who can't get along with a .400 hitter is crazy,"[17] said McCarthy, who not only changed his rules for the players, but also for himself. As for Williams, Ted would eventually come to regard McCarthy as the best manager he ever played for, respecting Marse Joe in large part because of his businesslike approach to the game.

During the 1948 season, the Red Sox, Cleveland Indians, and New York Yankees emerged as the three best teams in the American League. With the trio of rivals fighting for supremacy atop the league standings, there existed the very real possibility of a three-way tie at the end of the year. As the season moved into its second-to-last day, the Indians found themselves in first place, with the Red Sox and Yankees each a single game behind.

As fate would have it, the Yankees were scheduled to start a season-ending series against the Red Sox on Saturday, October 2. When the Red Sox defeated the Yankees to push them two games out, they mathematically eliminated the Pinstripers from contention. The following day, the Red Sox won again, giving them three straight wins to end the regular season, including a pair of victories against the dreaded Yankees. Bolstered by the trio of timely victories, the resilient Red Sox continued to put pressure on the first-place Indians. Williams had certainly played a significant role, with 2-for-2, 2-for-2, and 2-for-4 contributions against the pitching staffs of Washington and New York, respectively.

Meanwhile, the Indians won their game against the Tigers on Saturday to maintain a one-game lead. With Sunday the last day remaining on the regular season schedule, the Indians needed only to win their final game to clinch the pennant.

That win did not figure to come easily, not with future Hall-of-Famer Hal Newhouser on the mound for the Tigers. Newhouser allowed only five hits and out-pitched another Cooperstown immortal, Bob Feller, in saddling the Indians with a 7–1 loss. Coupled with the Red Sox 10–5 pounding of the Yankees, the defeat dropped the Indians into a first-place tie, each team sporting a record of 96–58.

In contrast to the National League's constitution, the American League's rules called for a one-game play-off (not a best two-out-of-three affair, as the Brooklyn Dodgers and St. Louis Cardinals had undergone in 1946, or as the Dodgers and New York Giants would experience memorably in 1951) to break any ties between teams at season's end. Since the Red Sox had won a coin flip conducted by American League President Will Harridge on September 24, they would enjoy the benefit of hosting the single play-off game at Fenway Park.

In the tie-breaking game against the Indians, the Red Sox prepared to meet Indians ace Bob Lemon, a future Hall-of-Famer; "I don't care if he's beaten us twenty times this year," Williams exclaimed the day before the game. "We'll knock his brains out tomorrow."[18]

The Red Sox, however, wouldn't receive that opportunity, as both managers made surprising choices in determining their starters for the tie-breaking game. Much to the surprise of Williams and his Boston teammates, the Indians decided not to start Lemon. Indians player-manager Lou Boudreau tabbed rookie Gene Bearden, despite the fact that he had started only two days earlier and would thus be pitching on one day's rest. Red Sox skipper Joe McCarthy made an even more stunning choice: journeyman Denny Galehouse, a 36-year-old right-hander who had posted a mediocre record of 8–7. More than a few Red Sox followers wondered why "Marse Joe" hadn't selected ace left-hander Mel Parnell, a fifteen-game winner whose credentials seemed much stronger than those of Galehouse.

Pitching in front of a capacity crowd of 33,957 curious observers, Galehouse ran into almost immediate first-inning trouble. After retiring the first two batters, Galehouse surrendered a home run to Lou Boudreau. The hard-hitting shortstop reached the screen atop Fenway's 37-foot-high wall, the famed "Green Monster" or simply "The Wall," in left field.

The Red Sox countered quickly against the youthful Bearden. With one out in the bottom of the first, Johnny Pesky doubled to right-center field and came home to score on Vern Stephens' single down the left-field line. The game remained tied through the first three innings.

In the top of the fourth, Galehouse ran into more trouble in facing Boudreau. The Indians' star shortstop singled and then moved up to second on Joe Gordon's hit. Galehouse now faced Ken Keltner, the Indians' star third baseman who was best known for stopping Joe DiMaggio's fifty-six-game hitting streak with two spectacular plays afield. This time, Keltner did considerable damage with his bat, planting a three-run home run beyond the outer reaches of Fenway. The long ball gave the Tribe a 4–1 lead and knocked Galehouse from the game in favor of veteran Ellis Kinder.

Kinder fared no better than Galehouse. He promptly allowed a double to Larry Doby, who eventually came around to score on Jim Hegan's infield grounder. The Indians now led by 4 runs.

The Indians scored another run in the fifth on Boudreau's second home run, but the Red Sox showed signs of life in the bottom of the sixth. Taking advantage of Joe Gordon's mishandling of a Williams pop-up, Bobby Doerr launched a two-out, two-run homer. The error-assisted rally brought the Red Sox within three runs.

The Sox remained within striking distance until the eighth, when Larry Doby doubled against Kinder and scored on an error by Williams, who failed to handle a long fly ball by Bearden. The Indians added another run in the top of the ninth, giving Bearden an 8–3 lead heading to the bottom of the ninth. Perhaps unprepared for the offerings of the first-year pitcher, the Red Sox had managed to do little damage against Bearden. Showing no signs of fatigue, Bearden shut down the Red Sox in the ninth to finish off a complete-game victory, an impressive feat against an intimidating lineup that included names like Dom DiMaggio, Doerr, Stephens, and Williams.

Unfortunately, Williams could not carry the Red Sox to victory in their final game. He had paced the Boston offense much of the season, leading the American League in batting (.369), on-base percentage (an amazing .497), slugging percentage (.615), walks (126), and doubles (44). Based purely on offensive numbers, Williams seemed like a lock for American League MVP honors. Instead, all it earned him was a third-place finish in the voting—and a distant third at that. While Lou Boudreau picked up the MVP with 324 points and Joe DiMaggio finished second with 213, Williams settled for a mere 171 points. When Williams found out further details about the voting, he seethed. None of the writers saw fit to place him first on the ballot.

While many of the beat writers didn't seem to fully appreciate Williams' value as a player, his teammates certainly did. They recognized him as a superstar—not just based on physical ability, but on hard work and practice. His work ethic impressed many of the Red Sox, even their pitchers. "He had amazing natural ability, but so do lots of guys," said Mel Parnell, the ace of the Red Sox staff and a winner of forty games during the 1948 and 1949 seasons. "He worked hard every day. He always took extra batting practice. He'd walk around all day holding a bat, just to keep the feel right. He treated batting practice just like [it was] a game. He would get enraged at himself for grounding out to third base in batting practice. That's what made him so good."[19]

Williams' work ethic continued into his thirties; if anything, he pushed himself harder as he moved into baseball's equivalent of middle age. In 1949, the entire Red Sox team played hard in putting on a late push for the pennant, winning eleven straight games in September to temporarily take the lead from the Yankees. As much as any Red Sox player, Williams played a huge role during that stretch, hitting four game-winning home runs as part of the eleven-game win streak.

The Yankees, however, quickly regained the lead in the American League, forcing the Red Sox back to a second-place standing. The Sox eventually regained the lead, remaining alive until the final days of the 1949 season, as they prepared to play the final two games of the season at Yankee Stadium on October 1 and 2. With a one-game lead in the standings, the Red Sox needed to win just one of the two games in order to cinch the pennant.

In the first game, a slap-hitting outfielder named Johnny Lindell decided the game for the Yankees by hitting a surprising home run in the bottom of the eighth. Lindell's blast landed in the left field bleachers, well beyond the reach of a frustrated Williams.

In the series finale, more slap-hitting Yankees stepped up and assumed the role of Red Sox–killer. In the first inning, Phil Rizzuto, a fine player but hardly a power hitter, boosted a drive that landed beyond the reach of Williams in left field. Landing on third with a triple, Rizzuto was brought home by teammate Tommy Henrich. Later in the game, the Red Sox dream ended when Jerry Coleman launched a three-run double—the decisive margin in New York's 5–3 win over Boston. The Yankee victory clinched the pennant for the Pinstripers, while ensuring that the Red Sox would not capture the league championship for a second straight season. The pair of wrenching games left Williams disconsolate. "When they were over," Williams said, "I just wanted to go and hide somewhere."[20] In later years, Williams would reflect on those two games at Yankee Stadium, referring to the pair of losses as the biggest disappointment of his career.[21]

Williams would not be able to find much solace in individual numbers either, as he went 0-for-2 against Vic Raschi in the finale and fell short of the AL batting title, losing out to George Kell of the Tigers. In determining the league-leading batting average that season, statisticians needed to calculate Kell's and Williams' marks to the fourth digit. Kell, with an average of .3429, barely beat out Williams at .3427. The narrow defeat in the batting race prevented Williams from claiming the Triple Crown. Still, Williams did lead the league in both home runs and RBIs—reaching a career high with 159 runs batted in—marking another hallmark season in a long line of sustained excellence.

In looking at his previous finishes in the MVP voting, Ted didn't expect much better come the winter of 1949. After hitting .406 one season and winning the Triple Crown in another, yet failing to garner the MVP nod either time, Ted decided not to wait by the phone for another disappointing MVP result. So he packed his bags and traveled to the Superior National Forest in Arkansas, where he planned to relax by taking part in an extended fishing expedition. During his stay in the forest, Williams received a phone call from his business manager, Fred Corcoran.[22] To Williams' amazement, he had received thirteen first-place votes and sufficient support for second, third and fourth-place, enough to walk away with the Most Valuable Player. With 272 points, Williams easily outdistanced Phil Rizzuto's 175 points. Rizzuto's Yankees might have finished higher than Williams' Red Sox in the standings, but the writers—for the first time since 1946—had acknowledged Ted's superior value to his team.

At the start of the 1950 season, Williams marked the beginning of his third decade in the major leagues. The new season also produced one of the uglier episodes of Williams' career. Playing in the first game of a doubleheader against the Tigers on May 11, Williams dropped a fly ball in short left field. The obvious error prompted fans in the left-field corner at Fenway Park to react with boos and heckles. Rather than ignore the disenchanted fans, Williams turned to face them, placing his thumbs in his ears. He then waved his hands, his way of mimicking a donkey and sending his own message of discontent to the crowd.[23]

In the eighth inning, Williams stepped to the plate with the bases loaded and lofted a long fly ball toward right field. Detroit's Vic Wertz tried to make the catch over his shoulder, but the ball clanged off his glove and bounced into the stands, giving Williams the cheapest of grand slams. Yet, the home run did little to soothe the fans. Instead, it only angered them, resulting in a growing cascade of boos against Williams.

The booing continued into the second game. As the Red Sox protected a 3–1 lead in the eighth, the Tigers loaded the bases, bringing Wertz back onto center stage. Wertz lined a single to left, which Williams charged and attempted to field quickly in an effort to cut off the tying run at the plate. As Williams approached, the ball took an unexpected hop and skidded past him toward the left-field wall. Rather than pursue the ball swiftly, a frustrated Williams jogged lazily toward the wall and then lobbed the ball back toward the infield. Three runs scored, giving the Tigers the lead and supplying the Fenway fans—especially those occupying the left-field corner—with more venom for Williams.

At the end of the inning, Williams ran in toward the Red Sox dugout. The fans in the grandstand offered their disapproval of his lackadaisical play. Instead of ignoring their wrath, Williams bent his elbow backward toward him and opened the palm of his other hand—completing a distasteful and unsportsmanlike gesture.[24]

Williams' callous on-field behavior produced a firestorm of criticism throughout Boston. Fans wondered about his lack of effort, while questioning his character and seeming lack of appreciation for the average Boston commoner. The criticism against Williams became so intense that he felt it necessary to make a public apology the next day.

On June 8, Williams took part in an historic thrashing of an American League rival, as the Red Sox established a major league record for the most runs in one game. Playing at Fenway Park, the Red Sox ripped the St. Louis Browns, 29–4. Williams and Red Sox first baseman Walt Dropo each hit 2 home runs, while Ted's good friend, Bobby Doerr, slammed three home runs and drove in eight of the Red Sox runs.

Williams' performance against the Browns marked one of the high points of the 1950 season. The low point occurred during the All Star Game, which should have been an occasion to celebrate another fine season in progress. During the pregame workout, Ted took some time to talk to National League slugger Ralph Kiner, representing the Pittsburgh Pirates in the Midsummer Classic. Little did Ted know, but he and Kiner would also become inescapably linked during the game.

In the first inning, Kiner pounded a pitch from Vic Raschi deep toward the gap in left center field. Making an immediate move on the ball, Williams tracked it toward the scoreboard, located at the base of the unpadded left-field wall. As Williams raced back, he lunged high for the ball, somehow snaring it in his glove as his arm hit the wall. In making an acrobatic catch to rob Kiner of a certain extra-base hit, Williams also drove his left elbow awkwardly into the scoreboard. Williams knew that he had injured his arm, which felt sore, but didn't consider it a serious setback. After grabbing his elbow in pain, he soon straightened out his body and tossed the ball back in toward the infield.

American League manager Casey Stengel asked Ted how he felt and whether he wanted to come out of the game. Minimizing the injury, Williams refused to leave the game. The AL trainer gave Williams' arm a quick rubdown, as a way of testing the condition of the elbow. Williams told the trainer that he felt well enough to continue playing.[25]

In the third inning, Kiner and Williams staged a near repeat of the first-inning incident. Kiner lined a pitch into left field and Williams made another excellent running catch, this time well away from the danger of the outfield wall. Two innings later, Williams gave little indication that the elbow hurt him as he stepped to the plate against Don Newcombe and singled, giving the American League the lead.

In the eighth inning, Williams again took his turn in the batter's box. This time, he struck out. As he swung and missed, he felt the pain in his left elbow worsen. The pain intensified so much that Ted finally left the game, which the American League eventually lost in 14 innings, 4–3. More importantly, a postgame examination revealed a fracture of Williams' elbow.

Remarkably, Williams had managed to play nearly an entire game with a broken elbow. His threshold for pain and his stern determination impressed many followers of the game and "gave many fans a new perspective on the Boston Red Sox slugger," according to the *Sporting News*.[26] In its next issue, the "Bible of Baseball" praised Williams for his All Star Game perseverance: "Ted has always regarded selection to the American League All-Star team as an honor and has contributed some of the most sparkling individual performances in the history of the midsummer classic. His attitude is in contrast with that of some other players who in previous years came up with excuses that enabled them to avoid participation in the inter-league contest. . . . The courage Ted displayed will add to his following, but it seems a tough way for anyone to have to prove his hustle and gameness."[27] Those aspects of Ted's character had sometimes been questioned in the past, but not in the summer of 1950.

On July 13, Williams underwent an operation in a Cambridge hospital to remove several bone fragments from his elbow. The injury was serious enough to warrant concern that Williams would miss the balance of the season. In fact, some writers speculated that doctors considered the fracture so severe that it might end Williams' career entirely. Ted worried that the writers might be right. Like the doctors, Williams was uncertain about his ability to resume playing.[28]

Still, Ted worked hard to rehabilitate his arm. Determined to make an in-season comeback, Ted would eventually return from the injury and would hit .350 over the second half to finish the season at a more-than-respectable .317. Yet, in Ted's mind, he felt that he never hit as well after the elbow injury as he had in all of the seasons leading up to 1950. Williams maintained that he could not extend his arm any more than 90 percent of its original capability, making him more susceptible to outside pitches and diminishing his overall power.[29] With Williams missing games and not playing at his previously established superstar level, the Red Sox finished third in the American League pennant race.

The early stages of the 1951 season brought a nostalgic dose of history to Fenway Park. In May, a group of nearly thirty old-time players visited the Red Sox home field to help celebrate the fiftieth anniversary of the American League. The list of legends included former Boston great Cy Young, the all-time leader in wins with 511, who visited with Williams prior to the scheduled game that day. Another visitor was Ty Cobb, whom some baseball historians regarded as the game's greatest hitter—at least prior to Ted's arrival. During a memorable pre-game visit with Williams, Cobb suggested that Ted try to hit the ball more often toward left field.[30] It was a piece of advice that Ted had heard often from those who thought he should take advantage of the Boudreau Shift, but this time the advice carried more a bit more weight (although Williams continued to try to pull the ball on most occasions). After all, Cobb had retired as major league baseball's leading hitter for average, with a career mark of .366. He knew a little something about hitting.

Williams remembered vividly his meetings with Cobb. "I never did train with Ty Cobb," Williams said in an interview with the Hall of Fame, "but I sure had a chance to talk with him quite a bit. He was a strict guy; he was a tough guy. . . . He and [Rogers] Hornsby were probably the two greatest outside of Babe Ruth, of course. [Cobb] wanted everybody to know how good he was and he wanted everybody to know how smart he was. There was no question he studied what he did and how he had to do it the best way and the most terrific way he could do it. I don't think [his lifetime batting average] will ever be matched."[31]

Beyond hitting, Williams respected Cobb for his all-around abilities and approach to the game. "Cobb was so fast, so big, he was a big guy and he was strong," Williams recalled fondly. "He had more ginger in his butt than [any] of the boys. He was probably as hard a player and put [out] as much every day as any player that ever played; I think Pete Rose is a little like that, too."[32]

Williams enjoyed another typically outstanding season in 1951, but that didn't prevent the Red Sox from reportedly considering a trade of their most talented player. With the Sox once again relegated to also-ran position in the American League pennant race and the team looking for better defensive play up the middle, Red Sox management talked to the Chicago White Sox about a possible swap of stars. According to one rumored deal, the Red Sox thought about trading Williams to the White Sox for shortstop Chico Carrasquel.[33] Though a mediocre-to-weak hitter, Carrasquel possessed a flair for fielding rivaled by few shortstops. The first Latino player selected to start an All Star Game, he possessed soft hands and dazzling range, causing some baseball historians to label him an early version of Luis Aparicio and Ozzie Smith, both Hall of Fame shortstops. Yet, Carrasquel's lack of hitting, coupled with the absence of the prodigious Williams from Boston's everyday lineup, likely would have hurt the Red Sox more than it would have helped. This was one trade that Red Sox management was better off for not making.

With their nucleus of stars intact, the Red Sox contended for much of the summer. They were considered the favorites by much of the national media, but they encountered stumbling blocks, including serious back problems for Bobby Doerr. As a team, the Red Sox slumped in September. One late-season game at Yankee Stadium epitomized Boston's frustrations. On September 28, the Yankees' Allie Reynolds kept the Red Sox hitless for the first eight and two-thirds innings. With one out to go, Williams popped up a Reynolds pitch, seemingly an easy play in foul territory for Yankee catcher Yogi Berra. Usually sure-handed, Berra dropped the ball. Given a second chance, most fans expected Williams to make Berra pay and end the no-hit bid with a solid line drive to an unmanned gap on the field. Instead, Williams popped up again, to nearly the same spot as the first pop-up. This time, Berra made the catch. A few days later, the Red Sox officially completed their disappointing third-place finish, as they settled for another also-ran conclusion to a season that had once seemed so promising.

It was yet another frustrating finish to a season for Williams, who had experienced more than his fare share of team disappointments since returning to the ballfields after his revolving-door tour through the military. The 1951 season also saw the end of the line for one of Williams' best friends on the Red Sox, the well-liked Bobby Doerr. Continuing back problems forced the future Hall-of-Famer to retire. The loss of Doerr left Williams without one of his closest allies in the clubhouse and left the Red Sox without a quality second baseman, while lessening the depth of their once-frightful batting order. That lineup would soon suffer another major loss, but not because of physical ailments like Doerr's. For the second time in the last decade, the Red Sox pivotal star would find his career interrupted by the forces of the political and military world.

NOTES

1. Interview with Ted Williams, conducted by Jeff Idelson of the National Baseball Hall of Fame, 2000.

2. Ibid.

3. Ibid.

4. John Updike, "Hub Fans Bid Kid Adieu," *The New Yorker*, October 22, 1960, 109.

5. Correspondence with Bill Nowlin, 2003.

6. Pietrusza et al., *Baseball*, 1237.

7. Riley, *The Red Sox Reader*, 60.

8. Interview with Ted Williams, conducted by Jeff Idelson of the National Baseball Hall of Fame, 2000.

9. Williams, with Pietrusza, *Teddy Ballgame*, 62.

10. Ibid.

11. Dan Shaughnessy, *The Curse of the Bambino* (New York: EP Dutton Books, 1990).

12. Eric Enders, *100 Years of the World Series* (New York: Barnes and Noble Books, 2003), 111.

13. Williams, with Pietrusza, *Teddy Ballgame*, 69.

14. Henry Berry, *Baseball's Greatest Teams: The Boston Red Sox* (New York: Collier, 1975), 148.

15. Interview with Ted Williams, conducted by Jeff Idelson of the National Baseball Hall of Fame, 2000.

16. Ibid.

17. Smith, *Storied Stadiums*, 171.

18. Ibid., 172.

19. Bruce Chadwick and David T. Spindel, *The Boston Red Sox: Memories and Mementoes of New England's Team* (New York: Abbeville Press, 1992), 49, 53.

20. Smith, *Storied Stadiums*, 199.

21. Berry, *Baseball's Greatest Teams,* 148.

22. Williams, with Pietrusza, *Teddy Ballgame*, 178.

23. Linn, "Growing Up With Ted," 56.

24. Ibid., 79.

25. Williams, with Pietrusza, *Teddy Ballgame*, 82.

26. "Ted Wins Recognition Hard Way," *Sporting News*, July 26, 1950, 12.

27. Ibid.

28. Williams, with Pietrusza, *Teddy Ballgame*, 83.

29. Bob Ryan, "Ted Williams: A Life Remembered—His Desire Made Wish Come True," *Boston Globe*, July 6, 2002, online edition.

30. Williams, with Pietrusza, *Teddy Ballgame*, 91.

31. Interview with Ted Williams, conducted by Jeff Idelson of the National Baseball Hall of Fame, 2000.

32. Ibid.

33. Wendel, *The New Face of Baseball*, 75.

Assuming the role of fighter pilot during the Korean War, Williams eyes the camera as he prepares for takeoff. *National Baseball Hall of Fame Library, Cooperstown, N.Y.*

6

WAR IS HELL—PART TWO

After the 1951 season, Williams once again found his playing career interrupted by the realities of American politics. In January of 1952, the U.S. Marines announced that they would recall Williams, a reserve in the Marine Corps, into active duty to serve in the Korean War. Once he passed his physical, Williams started the 1952 season knowing that he would not be able to finish it.

The military's decision surprised many observers, including Williams. Given Williams' age (33 at the time) and his previous tenure in World War II, Williams seemed like a logical candidate to be bypassed for military service in the latest war effort. Bitter over what he considered unfair treatment, which he felt was motivated by his sports celebrity status, Williams kept quiet about his displeasure and committed himself to a second stint in the military.[1] Williams, outfielder Bob Kennedy, and infielder Jerry Coleman would become the only major leaguers to serve during both World War II and the Korean War.

On April 30, 1952, the Red Sox decided to honor their two-time military participant with a special day at Fenway Park. They invited both the governor of Massachusetts and the mayor of Boston to attend "Ted Williams Day," giving the event a feeling of added importance.[2] During elaborate and emotional pregame ceremonies, Williams stood next to a young man named Fred Wolfe, a Korean War veteran confined to a wheelchair. Holding hands with the disabled veteran while holding back his own tears, Williams pondered the potentially devastating losses created by a war that he was about to enter himself.

In spite of the looming commitment to the military effort, the Red Sox did their best to keep the event upbeat. The Red Sox gave Williams a commemorative watch while rewarding his daughter, Barbara Joyce (nicknamed "Bobby Jo"), with a new bicycle. As an added touch, the Red Sox presented Ted with a motion picture projector, a new Cadillac, and a special memory book signed by 400,000 fans from around the country, along with all of the members of both the Red Sox and the visiting Detroit Tigers. Ted seemed most affected by the memory book, given the numbers of fans—even non-Red Sox fans—who had taken the time to sign it.[3] The array of gifts certainly surprised Williams, who had asked the Red Sox to keep the number of presents to a minimum.[4] With rumors swirling that Williams was about to play his last game (based on the premise that he would retire after the war), Fenway fans seranaded him with a rendition of *Auld Lang Syne*.

As part of the ceremony, Williams addressed the capacity crowd at Fenway Park. "This is the greatest day of my life," said an overwhelmed Williams. "I'll always remember it. It is a day every ballplayer looks for, and one I thought I'd never have. I never thought that when I came to the Red Sox organization fourteen years ago that they were such a wonderful organization. They've been wonderful to me."[5] At the end of his talk, Williams removed his cap from his head and waved it to the crowd.

Then, Williams gave the fans something by which they would remember him (besides the commemorative "Ted Williams Day" programs they received). In the first inning, he crossed up the Boudreau shift used by the Tigers and slapped a single toward the vacated hole at shortstop. And then came the true Williams' gift for his fans, provided in the seventh inning. With the score tied at 3–3 and two men out, Williams planted a long home run into the right-field bleachers, over that area known as "Williamsburg." The home run, delivered against Dizzy Trout, occurred in his final at-bat of the day—his final at-bat before his departure for war. With many fans convinced that the 33-year-old Williams had played his final major league game, they could take some small consolation in knowing that the two-run shot had given the first-place Red Sox the winning margin in a 5–3 victory.

Wins and losses, standings in the American League, and World Series possibilities all seemed fairly trivial in comparison with the real-life duties that lie ahead. As a pilot in Korea, Williams would face far more dangerous situations than he had faced while stateside during World War II. As his principal duty, he would have to fly numerous missions into enemy territory.

In one of his first missions, Williams received an assignment to fly deep into North Korea. On February 16, 1953, Williams followed orders to fly to a place called Kyomipo, located near the capital of North Korea. Flying at very low heights, he would have to drop anti-personnel weapons directly on the enemy.

The directives of the mission forced him to fly so low that it placed him within easy target of enemy fire. As he concentrated on hitting his own targets, Williams' Pantherjet fighter was struck by small arms fire, which penetrated one of the plane's hydraulic lines. "I made it over the target and dropped my bombs, and then I felt the plane mush up on me for an instant," Williams recalled.[6] The damage to the hydraulic line caused the plane to shake, making it difficult for Williams to keep control of the pilot's stick. "I didn't know I was hit until my [pilot's] stick got stiff and I knew I had lost my hydraulic system. Then the entire electrical system went out on me—no radio, no fuel or speed gauges. No nothing."[7] Williams attempted radio communications as an immediate way of seeking help, but received no answers in return.

Fortunately, another American plane came up to assist Williams. It was piloted by a man named Larry Hawkins, a lieutenant in the Marine Corps. Hawkins signaled for the distressed pilot to eject himself from his plane, but Williams couldn't understand the directions. Hawkins then tried an alternate approach, one that was generally followed by pilots who had been hit, instructing Williams to lift the plane to a higher altitude. Williams properly interpreted that piece of advice and did as Hawkins indicated. Hawkins successfully guided Williams out of the line of continued fire, toward the Yellow Sea, and then back toward land.[8] There was no time to get back to their base, so Hawkins pointed Ted in the direction of a nearby Air Force Base.[9] It was there that he would have to attempt a crash landing.

As Williams approached the airfield, one of the plane's wheel doors suddenly exploded. The noise stunned Williams, who nonetheless continued his descent at over 200 miles per hour—twice the recommended speed on a landing attempt. Barely controlling the plane, Williams prepared for a wild crash landing, even though he knew he couldn't lower his wheels. He hit the ground running, at his own estimate of 225 miles an hour. The plane went into an immediate skid, and continued to skid for a stretch that seemed endless. "Nothing worked, no dive brakes, flaps, nothing to slow up the plane," said Williams, who watched people on the ground try to scatter and avoid the wreckage of the jet. "I could see Koreans running wildly in all directions."[10] As Williams futilely applied the brakes, he barely avoided a pair of fire trucks stationed at the airfield. Finally, after skidding for over 2,000 feet, the plane came to a grinding halt.[11]

Knowing that the plane would explode once the fire hit the fuel tanks,[12] Williams struggled to escape from the cockpit. Initially, he couldn't pry himself free. After several moments of struggle, he finally lifted his body from the cockpit and out of the plane, diving onto the ground outside. Several rescue workers helped distance him from the plane, which quickly caught fire. Within a few moments, the entire plane was engulfed in flames. It burned completely, as Williams watched from safety.[13]

Unbelievably, Williams escaped the entire incident—the enemy hit and the fiery crash landing—without significant injury. Other than minor cuts and scratches, Williams escaped unharmed. Yet, he freely admitted the feelings of terror that such an air mission caused him. "Scared to death," Williams revealed to the Hall of Fame, "[I was] holding on. I sat in the cockpit, and I said, 'If there's anybody up there that could help me, now's the time to do it.' I did say that."[14]

Williams felt safer and more comfortable flying jets, rather than any other types of military aircraft. "I requested jets," Williams recalled. "A friend of mine had been in Korea. Old Marine buddy, one of my great friends, Bill Churchman. He said that he'd been there . . . [that] the jets were better for what we were doing. So I requested jets—can't guarantee a thing—but that's what I was trying to get. So I applied for jets and I got jets, which was a break for me."[15] Williams received another break when he was given the opportunity to serve as wingman for John Glenn, who would later gain fame as the first American astronaut to orbit the Earth.

Given the severity of the Kyomipo incident and crash, Ted might have appreciated some time off. That wouldn't happen. With the Marine Corps short of fighter pilots, Williams returned to the air the next day. He flew a mission over Seoul, this time without incident. A few months later, he flew a mission that brought him over a location named Chinnampo. As he flew over Chinnampo, his plane was struck once again, not by ground fire but by anti-aircraft fire. Thankfully, the damage to the plane was not nearly as severe as the previous incident. Williams returned to the ground with little trouble.[16]

Unrelated to the latest onslaught of enemy fire, Williams came down with a nagging case of respiratory problems, brought upon by a bout with pneumonia. Forcing him into a military hospital, the illness also affected his inner ear and his hearing. (The loss of hearing would help explain why Williams sometimes talked with such a loud and booming voice; he felt a need to do so in order to hear himself.)[17] With his condition sufficiently weakened and his damaged ear preventing him from flying, the military shipped Williams off to Hawaii.[18] There he would receive more advanced treatment for his inner ear trouble.

While in Honolulu, the military decided that the ailing Williams was no longer in proper condition to fly combat missions. Ted received his orders to return home, his tour of duty ended. Unlike his turn in World War II, his second tour had proved more memorable and far more dangerous. By the end of his second stint in the military, Williams had flown a total of thirty-nine missions, including that horrific crash landing near Kyomipo.

When he emerged from his tour of duty in Korea, Williams felt especially fortunate.

> I got to say this, how lucky I've been in life. I know how lucky I've been in life more than anybody will ever know. I've lived a kind of precarious life style, precarious in sports, flying, and baseball. So anyway, I know how lucky I've been. But the [one of the] things I'm proudest of in my life is that I became a Marine pilot, I worked hard. I wasn't prepared to go into that, until I got into it and then I had to work hard as hell to keep going to keep up. I did have reasonable flying abilities. . . . I think that was the greatest accomplishment I had in my life.[19]

With his war duties ended, Williams now considered his future in baseball.

Ted did not want to retire. He definitely wanted to return; it was merely a matter of when that comeback would begin. At first, Ted considered the possibility of not playing the second half of the 1953 season. He was still worn out from his tour of duty and his subsequent stay in the hospital. As Williams considered the pros and cons of returning in midseason, Commissioner Ford C. Frick asked him to throw out the ceremonial first pitch at the All Star Game, which Ted did. It was an honor afforded few active players, instead reserved mostly for retired stars and non-baseball celebrities. Fans at Cincinnati's Crosley Field treated Ted to a standing ovation, partly in appreciation for his military work and partly in anticipation that he would play baseball again. The reaction of the crowd in Cincinnati convinced Williams that it was time to return.[20]

On August 6, 1953, Williams made his first appearance with the Red Sox after his heroic military stint in Korea. Like his experience in Cincinnati, Williams received a rousing response from the hometown fans, who had sometimes expressed their displeasure with Boston's resident superstar. Now the favored son, but without the benefit of spring training or any kind of normal preseason regimen, Ted did his best to readjust to the requirements of hitting a baseball. His timing off, Williams popped out in his 1953 debut, a pinch-hitting attempt. Yet, he would fare much better in subsequent at-bats that season. Three days after first at-bat, Williams delivered a pinch-hit home run against Cleveland's standout starter, Mike Garcia. The home run traveled an estimated 420 feet.

Ten days later, Lou Boudreau, formerly an opponent and rival of the Red Sox but now the Boston manager after being hired at the conclusion of the

1951 season, penciled Williams' name onto the lineup card for the first time. Williams responded by smacking a double and a home run in front of a crowd of over 25,000 fans at Fenway Park. Williams' first start provided a portent of good things to come. Although Williams would fall well short of the requisite number of plate appearances to qualify for the American League's batting title, he would finish the season with a .407 batting average. He would also hit 13 home runs in only 91 at-bats for the fourth-place Red Sox, helping him accumulate a slugging percentage of .901. Williams' ability to hit immediately for both average and power, after a lengthy and arduous stint in the Korean War that had cost him the better part of two seasons, amazed most observers of the game.

In regaining his timing so quickly, Williams had managed a remarkable return. He would have to undergo a comeback of a different sort in the spring of 1954. On March 1, Williams fractured his collarbone on the first day of spring training. The injury occurred as he dove for a ball hit by teammate Hoot Evers, one of Boston's outfielders. As Williams fell to the ground, he realized almost immediately that he had broken a bone. In response to the cracked collarbone, an orthopedic surgeon removed a piece of bone about an inch-and-a-half long, replacing it with a four-inch metal pin. As a result, Williams missed another Opening Day and the first thirty-six games of the regular season. He would not return to the Red Sox fold until early May.

On May 15, Williams returned by pinch-hitting. After flying out, he remained in the game and took another turn at bat, this time grounding harmlessly to shortstop. On the heels of an unimpressive return, Williams felt pain in his collarbone and had trouble sleeping. In spite of the pain, Williams fared much better the following day. Playing in a doubleheader against Detroit, Williams collected eight hits in nine at-bats. The barrage included a double, two home runs, and seven RBIs, but couldn't prevent a pair of losses to the Tigers.

The pain felt in his collarbone couldn't prevent Williams from staging a magnificent follow-up to his 1953 second-half performance. Williams batted .345, which would have earned him another American League batting crown if he had accrued a sufficient number of official at-bats. According to the rules of the day, a batter's eligibility for the batting crown was based on his total number of at-bats (which doesn't include walks), and not his total number of plate appearances (which does include walks). Since Williams' 129 walks didn't count as at-bats, he fell short of the required number. Williams considered the rule unfair, and baseball officials subsequently came to agree, later changing the requirement to plate appearances and not at-bats. (The rule came too late to help Williams, but would help batting champions of future generations, such as Barry Bonds.) As it was, Williams led the league in walks, on-base percentage, and slugging percentage, standing out as one of the few bright spots on a fourth-place also-ran that finished forty-two games out of first place.

The combination of on-field losing, pain from his repeated injuries, the frustration of frequents bouts with the flu and a variety of viruses, and a general feeling of wear and tear convinced Williams that it was time to step aside. He sat out the first month of the 1955 season, but his retirement turned out to be short-lived. He did not want to leave the game after such an injury-plagued, illness-shortened season, one that had left him with too little playing time—and too much disappointment.[21] Believing that he could still play well if healthy, he decided to return in May, and promptly picked up where he had left off in the batter's box, which remained an area of comfort for him. For the third straight year, he made the most out of a partial season of play. Once again overcoming an extended absence while remaining a beacon on a fourth-place team, Williams bounced back to hit .356 with a mammoth .703 slugging percentage.

Like all the Red Sox, Williams had to deal with the tragic loss of a teammate during the 1955 season. In May, promising young first baseman Harry Agganis came down with a case of pneumonia. Known as "The Golden Greek," he was hitting .313 at the time, but the illness knocked him from the lineup. The onset was so severe that he was forced into the hospital for a short stay. Agganis then returned to action, but quickly encountered a series of chest pains and high fevers. Doctors determined that he needed to be hospitalized for a second time. The Red Sox hoped that the return to the hospital would restore Agganis' health. It didn't. His condition only worsened. On June 27, Agganis experienced a blood clot and died unexpectedly at the age of 26.

It was a tragically new experience for Williams, who had never before dealt with the death of an active teammate. The sudden passing of Agganis served as a brutal warning to all of the Red Sox of the relative brevity of both their careers in baseball and their inhabitancies on this earth. Coupled with the deaths that Williams had witnessed first-hand during his harrowing tour in Korea, it may have reminded him that nothing was guaranteed—not the pennant, not the World Series, and not even the ability to fulfill a career.

NOTES

1. Williams, with Pietrusza, *Teddy Ballgame*, 96.
2. Greene, "Ted Williams' Ten Greatest Days," 26.
3. Ibid.
4. Williams, with Pietrusza, *Teddy Ballgame*, 93.
5. Ibid., 94.

6. Greene, "Ted Williams' Ten Greatest Days," 26.

7. Ibid.

8. Williams, with Pietrusza, *Teddy Ballgame*, 98.

9. Correspondence with Bill Nowlin, 2003.

10. Greene, "Ted Williams' Ten Greatest Days," 26.

11. Williams, with Pietrusza, *Teddy Ballgame*, 98.

12. Greene, "Ted Williams' Ten Greatest Days," 26.

13. Correspondence with Bill Nowlin, 2003.

14. Interview with Ted Williams, conducted by Jeff Idelson of the National Baseball Hall of Fame, 2000.

15. Ibid.

16. Williams, with Pietrusza, *Teddy Ballgame*, 99.

17. Shelby Whitfield, *Kiss It Goodbye* (New York: Abelard-Schuman, 1973), 22.

18. Williams, with Pietrusza, *Teddy Ballgame*, 99.

19. Interview with Ted Williams, conducted by Jeff Idelson of the National Baseball Hall of Fame, 2000.

20. Williams, with Pietrusza, *Teddy Ballgame*, 103.

21. Dreyspool, "Ted Williams," 58.

7

CONTROVERSY REPLACES COMEBACK

The Red Sox hoped to return to contention in 1956, with the outfield of Williams, the energetic Jimmy Piersall, and the multi-talented Jackie Jensen providing much of the basis for optimism. Acknowledged as one of the best outfields of the 1950s, the threesome supplied the Red Sox with a nucleus of solid hitting and, thanks to Piersall and Jensen, above-average defensive play. Unfortunately, the rest of the team fell short, resulting in another summer of mediocrity. The Red Sox finished fourth for the fourth consecutive season, well out of the money in the American League pennant race.

The 1956 season also represented one of the low points of Ted's often contentious relationship with the Fenway fans. In August, the Red Sox hosted the rival Yankees. Mickey Mantle popped a short fly into left field. Williams raced in from left field, grabbing the ball on the run, but couldn't hold on. When the ball popped out of his glove, some of the Boston fans began to boo. Later in the game, Williams once again bolted in search of a fly ball. Racing back toward the fence, Williams made a fine over-the-shoulder snatch, this time maintaining possession of the ball. Many of the fans responded by cheering Williams.

The fickle nature of the fans infuriated Ted, who had not mellowed, even in his late thirties. As he ran in from left field toward the dugout, Williams spit. A few moments later, he stopped, turned around, and spit in the direction of left field. He then followed that gesture by spitting in the direction of right field. Not done there, Williams again spit toward left field. He then spit for a fifth time, on this occasion in the dugout.[1] Unbelievably, Williams wasn't done in expressing himself. He stepped out of the dugout, spitting for a *sixth* time, this time on the playing field.[2] Many of the fans noticed his repeated gestures, reacting with a mix of cheers and boos.

Later in the game, Williams came up to the plate with the bases loaded and the game tied in the bottom of the ninth. In typical Williams fashion, he showed a selective eye at bat, and coaxed a game-winning walk. Yet, the walk did little to soothe an irritated Williams. Upset that he hadn't been able to swing the bat and deliver a game-ending hit, Williams flipped his bat in the air in frustration. Viewing his latest gesture as a manifestation of selfishness, some of the fans started to boo. The bat-flipping incident also drew the ire of the local media and of Red Sox owner Tom Yawkey, who announced a fine of $5,000. Even in victory, Williams had managed to touch the nerves of many within the Red Sox community.

Mired in controversy, Williams responded in typically grandiose fashion. Playing the first game of a road trip the following day, Williams powered a crucial home run in the top of the ninth inning, helping the Red Sox to a victory. Ted expected the fans in Baltimore's Memorial Stadium to boo him lustily, but they surprised him with a rousing ovation. Somehow, Williams' heroics had overcome his caustic behavior, managing to win the sentiments of even the enemy fans.

Williams remained charismatic as he settled into his late thirties; similarly, he retained a large portion of his hitting skills. By the start of the 1957 season, Williams was already 38 years old, but he seemed more youthful in the eyes of opposing pitchers. On June 13, the ageless Williams showed his sustained power at the plate by crushing three home runs in a 9–2 win over the Indians. Due to the cold weather in Cleveland that night, Williams had wanted to leave the blowout game after his second long ball, but manager Mike "Pinky" Higgins convinced him to keep playing, allowing him to hit another home run. It was not the first time that season that Williams had launched three home runs in one game; he had accomplished the same feat against the White Sox earlier that spring. Williams thus became the first American League player to hit three home runs in a game twice in the same season.

Williams sustained his power into September, even as he struggled from the effects of a heavy chest cold. In one stretch, he hit a record-tying four home runs in four consecutive at-bats, including a pinch-hit shot into Yankee Stadium's right-field bleachers against future Hall-of-Famer Whitey Ford. "I feel terrible," said a surprised Williams, "but every time I take a swing at the ball, it goes out of the park."[3] After hitting the fourth consecutive home run, the enemy crowd of over 34,000 fans, out of awe for what they had just seen, saw fit to give the Red Sox rival a wild ovation. He continued his heavy-hitting stretch with a single and a walk against Yankee pitching, and then delivered another single against Washington the following day. Combining singles, walks, and home runs, Williams had reached base in sixteen consecutive plate appearances.

The stretch against New York and Washington highlighted Ted's season. Williams not only hit for power in 1957, finishing second in the American League with 38 blasts, but managed to compile the second-highest batting average of his major league career. After flirting with a .400 batting average, Williams finished the season at .388, coming within eighteen percentage points of matching his 1941 mark. Williams' hitting looked even more impressive given his lack of speed; he managed only 12 infield hits that season, a relatively paltry number. By Williams' own estimation, if he possessed the foot speed that he did earlier in his career, he would have easily batted .400, and perhaps as high as .420.[4] (No other Red Sox player would come close to matching Williams' .388 average until Nomar Garciaparra would hit .372 in the year 2000; even so, Garciaparra fell sixteen points short of Williams' mark.) Just as significantly, Williams led the league in both on-base percentage, with a remarkable .528, and slugging percentage, with a stunning .731.

Such numbers seemed more than capable of propelling Williams to his second Most Valuable Player Award. Yet, the Red Sox also-ran status in the pennant race—a third-place finish in 1957—once again doomed Ted to runner-up status in the award voting. On November 22, the Baseball Writers' Association of America announced the results of the balloting: in one of the closest tallies ever, Mickey Mantle had barely edged Williams in the American League's MVP voting. Mantle gained 233 votes to Williams' 209 tallies. Mantle batted .365 with 34 home runs for the first-place Yankees, while Williams had toiled for the third-place Red Sox.

Mantle, a legendary player in his own right, often professed his admiration for Williams' abilities as a hitter. At times, Mantle felt like a scout, or at least a diehard fan, while observing Williams. "Whenever we'd play Boston, I'd get right up on the edge of the dugout steps when Williams was up and I'd study him," Mantle said. "I played with Joe D. [DiMaggio] and I admired Joe D., but I have to say Ted Williams is the best hitter I ever saw. He had tremendous hand-eye coordination, good bat speed, a great turn [of his hips], power, concentration. He had it all."[5]

While the baseball writers may not have showed similar appreciation for Williams' feats in the fall of 1957, others did. The *Sporting News* selected Williams as its Player of the Year and then continued to honor him by placing a drawing of him on the cover of *The Sporting News Official Guide for 1958.* The Red Sox also showed their appreciation for their longtime star. On February 6, 1958, Williams signed a one-year contract with Tom Yawkey's Red Sox.

Reports on the worth of the contract estimated from $125,000 to $150,000. Either way, Williams became the highest-paid player in the history of the franchise.

Unfortunately, the 1958 season would pose several obstacles for the soon-to-be 40-year-old Williams. During the spring, Williams sat down for a meal and ate some bad oysters, resulting in a case of ptomaine poisoning. After recovering from the illness, Williams experienced a series of injuries. At first, there was an injured ankle. He then pulled a muscle in his side. He also injured his wrist on two occasions. He came down with another viral infection, a problem that was becoming an annual rite of summer.

And then there was controversy, which never seemed to stray too far from Williams' side. During a game in September, Williams struck out looking, a cause of frustration. Upset with himself, Williams threw his bat away. He intended to throw the bat down—to the ground—but the bat stuck to his hand longer than expected and shot upward. By the time the bat had landed it had reached the stands, where it struck a 60-year-old woman named Gladys Heffernan in the head. As it turned out, she happened to be Joe Cronin's housekeeper, which only added to Ted's embarrassment. Fortunately, the bat did her no serious damage, but Williams rightly took his share of criticism for the show of temper. As a way of apologizing to Mrs. Heffernan, Williams purchased an expensive diamond watch and gave it to her as a Christmas present.[6]

The litany of controversy, illness, and injury didn't prevent Williams from making a run at the American League's batting title. He and another Red Sox player, the singles-hitting Pete Runnels, both found themselves in mid-season contention for the crown, along with Detroit's Harvey Kuenn, another line-drive hitter with little power. In July and August, the three veteran batters—a slugger and two contact hitters—battled for the title as the league's top batsman.

By September, Kuenn had fallen out of the race, leaving Runnels and Williams to decide the matter. With the Red Sox destined to finish a distant third that season, the competition between Runnels and Williams consumed much of the interest of Red Sox fans. Runnels took the lead in early September, taking aim on what would be his first batting title. During the final days of the season, Williams went on a tear, tying Runnels at .322 on September 26. The Red Sox now prepared to play their final series of the season, a set against the Senators in Washington. Appropriately enough, Runnels and Williams teamed up to hit back-to-back home runs in the first game of the series. Runnels finished the day 3-for-6, but Williams went 3-for-4 to take a lead of three points.

On the final day of the season, the Red Sox faced Washington's tough right-hander Pedro Ramos, who had a history of making life difficult for Williams at the plate. Runnels failed to pick up a hit in his first at-bat, but Williams surprised himself by clubbing a home run into the left-field bullpen. Later in the game, Williams added a double. In the meantime, Runnels went hitless in his next three at-bats to finish the game 0-for-4 and conclude the season at .322. That put him six points short of Williams, who had finished the season with seven hits in his last 11 at-bats, giving him a final mark of .328 and rightful claim to his sixth American League batting title—his first as a 40-year-old.

Runnels could have been excused for feeling disappointed, but he took some comfort in knowing that he had lost out to the best hitter of the era. "If I'd been beaten out by anyone else, I'd have felt bad," Runnels said after the final game. "But nobody but Ted could have beaten me in a race like this. It's no disgrace to finish second to Williams."[7]

With injuries becoming a common theme throughout his thirties and now into his early forties, Williams didn't figure to regain perfect health in 1959. Prior to reporting to the Red Sox new spring training camp in Arizona, Williams received permission to engage in some early workouts with the San Francisco Giants in Florida. As it turned out, he should have stayed home. While swinging a bat in an effort to loosen up his muscles, Williams felt a twinge in his neck. He thought it was only a minor problem, but the pain lingered. As it turned out, the latest injury to his neck dated back to an operation he had endured five years earlier.

Even after reporting to Arizona and beginning the exhibition season, Williams felt continued pain in his neck. If he swung and missed, the neck hurt considerably. Even when he swung and made contact, the neck still hurt. The Red Sox had no choice but to place Williams on the disabled list to start the season.

Williams remained sidelined until the second month of the season. Playing in his season debut on May 12, he went hitless in five at-bats. After the first week of the season, his batting average rested at an unaccustomed .045. It wasn't until the latter part of June that Ted managed to raise his average above the meager .200 mark.

Williams struggled so badly during the first half that he was eventually benched by manager Pinky Higgins. The reason for Ted's struggles was clear. It had little to do with age, and everything to do with a neck that remained stiff and sore. As the season progressed, the condition of Ted's neck improved slightly, allowing him to lift his batting average during the second half of the season. Still, he finished the season a meager .254, a simply unheard-of batting mark for a hitter of Williams' ilk. Embarrassed by his performance, Williams approached Red Sox management and demanded that his salary be cut from $125,000 to $90,000. Williams didn't have to ask for a paycut; few players ever have. Given his contributions over the years, it's unlikely that Tom Yawkey would have asked for such a salary cut, but Williams felt it was the appropriate thing to do.

While 1959 turned out to be the least productive season of Williams' major league career, it also evolved as one of the most socially and culturally significant seasons in the history of the Red Sox franchise—and showed Williams to be more than just a splendid player. It was the year that the Red Sox finally integrated their team, bringing a black infielder named Elijah "Pumpsie" Green up from the minor leagues on July 21. Green was a mediocre talent, a far cry from multi-skilled players like Jackie Robinson or Willie Mays, players the Red Sox could have signed in earlier years if the organization had been more open-minded and less racist. (Robinson had actually attended a Red Sox tryout during the 1940s, but the team's management showed indifference to his skills and treated the tryout as a farce, determined to keep the team completely white.) Perhaps because of Green's limited abilities, but probably more because of the color of his skin, Green's arrival in Boston was met with a combination of indifference and disdain. A full twelve years after Robinson had broken the color barrier, Green's debut seemingly brought little enlightenment to either the players or the front office.

Yet, Williams was one of the few Red Sox who went out of his way to treat Green well; he warmed up with him prior to games when other members of the Red Sox would not.[8] Williams participated in the pregame ritual partly because he wanted to make Green feel more comfortable in otherwise difficult circumstances.[9] It was the kind of behavior rarely exhibited by a superstar toward a utility infielder, whether black, white, or Latino. It was the kind of character that baseball had seen so little of since Harold "Pee Wee" Reese's courageous and rightful acceptance of Jackie Robinson as both a teammate and friend in the late 1940s. It was also a clear sign that there was far more to Ted Williams than the mere skill of hitting a baseball. While some of his critics had labeled him as selfishly obsessive in his pursuit of hitting perfection, Williams had actually succeeded in exhibiting more humanity and compassion than almost any member of the entire Red Sox organization.

NOTES

1. Williams, with Pietrusza, *Teddy Ballgame*, 115.
2. Ibid.
3. Updike, "Hub Fans Bid Kid Adieu," 109–110.
4. Berry, *Baseball's Greatest Teams*, 150.

5. Chadwick and Spindel, *The Boston Red Sox*, 45.
6. Williams, with Pietrusza, *Teddy Ballgame*, 126.
7. Greene, "Ted Williams' Ten Greatest Days," 26.
8. Bryant, *Shut Out*, 66.
9. Ibid.

A smiling Ted patiently awaits his turn at bat, circa 1958. He would take his final at-bat in 1960. *National Baseball Hall of Fame Library, Cooperstown, N.Y.*

8

A FINAL SEASON

Given Williams' kindly and concerned efforts with Pumpsie Green, it seemed only right that good fortune would await "Teddy Ballgame" in 1960. He emerged from spring training unscathed—no injuries, no bouts with the flu, no recalls into the military. With his neck healed and his body refreshed, Williams appeared primed for a comeback season.

Unfortunately, the 1960 season also brought tragedy to Ted and his family. His younger brother, Danny, who had grown up as a sickly child, was gravely ill. He had a form of leukemia, a cancer of the bone marrow, a condition so pervasive that routine actions caused only additional ailments. "He threw a ball or an orange at somebody," Ted explained, "and broke his damn arm."[1] That season, Danny Williams passed away. He was Ted's only sibling. In some direct way, Danny's death may have inspired Ted's continued passion for the Jimmy Fund, a Red Sox–supported charity aimed at helping children with cancer.[2] Williams had first become involved with the Jimmy Fund in the late 1940s. He would contribute hours upon hours in his efforts for the Jimmy Fund, both in raising money and in making personal visits to children suffering from various forms of cancer at the Dana-Farber Cancer Institute.

More cheerful events would come Ted's way in 1960, especially with regard to on-field achievements. In his first at-bat of the new season, Williams sent a message to opposing American League pitchers by nailing a home run, notable for both its distance and the pitcher that it victimized. Williams clubbed the lengthy home run against Washington's Camilo Pascual, regarded by some experts as the American League's best pitcher. The ball traveled over 450 feet, leading some longtime Williams observers to speculate that it was the longest home run of his career.

The 1960 schedule was unusual: The Red Sox played an "advance opener" in Washington before going home. The following day, Williams provided another sign that the struggles of the previous season might not reappear. Playing in the Fenway Park opener, Williams hit another home run, this time against a lesser pitcher named Jim Coates. With two home runs in two games, Williams seemed to have regained his touch for the long ball. And then, as he rounded the bases on the Coates home run, Williams felt tightness in his leg. The reason? He had pulled a leg muscle while simply jogging around the bases. The injury provided Williams with yet another reminder about the frailties of a body that counted 40-plus years.

The injury set Williams back for a few weeks, and just as his leg began to recover, he came down with another case of a viral infection. Ever since his days in Korea, the rather mysterious infection had afflicted him on almost an annual basis. As usual, doctors treated him with a variety of antibiotics, in the hopes that one would contain the infection. In the meantime, Red Sox manager Billy Jurges called upon Ted to play a reduced role as a pinch-hitter. When Williams failed in a couple of attempts off the bench, he began to give considerable thought to retirement.

Williams then started a game on June 5 against the Yankees. Facing right-hander Ralph Terry, Ted looked bad in striking out twice. In his third trip to the plate, Williams worked the count to 3-and-2 before launching a waist-high Terry fastball into the bullpen in right center field. The ball landed about 400 feet away from home plate, signaling the beginning of Williams' latest comeback from baseball oblivion.

Over the next two weeks, Williams hit 5 more home runs, giving him a total of 8 in only 15 starts. The most memorable home run occurred on June 17; that day Williams became the fourth major league player to hit 500 career home runs, joining Hall of Famers Babe Ruth, Jimmie Foxx, and Mel Ott in what was still a highly exclusive group. Williams' 2-run shot, coming against Indians right-hander Wynn Hawkins and clearing the left-field wall at Cleveland's Municipal Stadium, helped the Red Sox to a 3–1 win over the Indians. After the game, Williams returned to the Boston clubhouse, where he found that his teammates had posted a makeshift sign in tribute to his latest accomplishment. The crude, handwritten sign listed the names Ruth, Foxx, Ott, and Williams from top to bottom, with the number "500" indicated in quotations below Williams' name. Williams stood next to the sign, holding the 500th home-run ball, as cameramen snapped a series of historic pictures.[3]

Williams reached other important, though less glamorous, career milestones in 1960. He collected his 2,000th walk, confirming his supreme knowledge of the strike zone and his Job-like patience at the plate. He collected his 1,800th RBI, a milestone that corroborated his ability to produce runs, an ability that had sometimes been criticized. He also appeared in his sixteenth All Star Game, a testament to both his talents and his popularity.

In addition to milestones, mid-season awards came Ted's way in 1960. On August 17, the *Sporting News* named Williams "Player of the Decade" for the 1950s. It was a fitting honor for a player who had established himself as such a dominant force from 1950 to 1959. During that time span, he had won two batting titles, led the American League in slugging percentage twice, and also led the league in walks twice—all despite missing significant time while serving his country in battle.

The month of August also brought more pain to Williams' aging body. Towards the end of the month, Williams suffered a strain of his shoulder. The latest injury made it difficult for Williams to warm up prior to gametime, even during the hottest days of the season.[4] For the second time in 1960, Ted seriously considered retiring, coming close to making an official announcement.

Yet, Williams held off on any final decision or announcement. The Red Sox manager, Mike "Pinky" Higgins, who had replaced Billy Jurges in mid-season, convinced Williams of the moral importance of fulfilling his contract by continuing to earn his paycheck. In addition, Williams didn't want to depart the American League pennant race in midstream. Although the Red Sox had long since ceased being a factor in the race for the postseason, they still had several games remaining with both of the league's top contenders, the Baltimore Orioles and New York Yankees. Williams didn't feel it would be right to miss those games, not when he could play the role of "spoiler" against either team. Williams wanted either the Orioles or the Yankees to earn their way to the postseason, and he wanted them to earn it by having to pitch to him.

Williams kept quiet about the possibility of retirement and continued to play despite the pain in his shoulder and the age-induced stiffness throughout his body. His body, no longer rail thin as in his earlier days, now displayed some of the traits of a 40-year-old man, including added girth in his midsection. He played in series against both Baltimore and New York, doing his best despite his physical limitations. Always patient at the plate, he took more pitches than usual during the latter stages of the season, mostly because he could handle only inside pitches located between his waist and knees.[5]

In light of his advancing age, expanding waistline, and declining muscle skills, the waning days of the 1960 season placed Ted in an even more contemplative mood about his future. Shortly before the end of the season, the 42-year-old Williams finally decided to make a break with the National Pastime. Although he still possessed ample abilities at the plate, Ted had come to the conclusion that the wear and tear on his body had become too much. It was time for him to retire as an active player, effective at the end of the 1960 season.

On the afternoon of Wednesday, September 28, the Red Sox prepared to play their final home game of the season. Williams reported to the ballpark at about 10:50 in the morning, which was a particularly early arrival time for him.[6] With the Red Sox on their way to a seventh-place finish in the American League and in the throes of their worst season in nearly thirty years, the afternoon game at Fenway meant little on the surface; a crowd of only 10,454 attended the final home game. Yet, for Williams, who stopped only briefly at his locker before reporting to the trainer's room,[7] the game represented something quite special—and final. Even though the Red Sox still had three road games awaiting them on the schedule, Ted had apparently decided to end his playing career in Boston.[8] He would not travel with the team on its final road trip, instead completing his career in the ballpark he had called home since 1939. "Well, in the first place," Williams recalled in an interview with the Hall of Fame, "I wasn't going to play in New York [for the final series of the year] and I told them that. I said, I'm not going to New York and play the last three games. I said, we're out of the pennant [race] and I've had it, I just can't do it. So nobody said anything about it."[9] Williams hoped that his plan to end his career in Boston would remain secret, so that no one would create a spectacle of his final game. Williams told his friend, clubhouse attendant Johnny Orlando, about his intentions, and hoped that few others would find out about his plans. "The word got out," Williams explained. "[Broadcaster] Curt Gowdy always said he knew that was going to be my last game. Apparently, Johnny Orlando told him."[10] With Williams' plans now public, the American League honored Williams with its presence; league president Joe Cronin, formerly Ted's manager, made sure to attend the game and pay a special visit to the dugout, where he reminisced fondly with his former player.

Just about five minutes before one o'clock, and about thirty-five minutes prior to the scheduled start of the game, Williams made his way from the clubhouse to the dugout.[11] As he entered the dugout, he nearly bumped into one of the few reporters he considered a true friend, Bud Leavitt, the editor of the *Bangor Daily News*.[12] Almost simultaneously, a swarm of cameramen approached Williams from the playing field, forming a semi-circle around the soon-to-be-retired legend. Ted tried to shoo the reporters away, using some profanity in the process, so that he could continue his conversation with Leavitt.[13]

After the media had been cleared from the dugout area, the Red Sox staged a simple but extremely emotional ceremony and retired the uniform no. 9 of the most recognizable player in the history of their franchise. Red Sox broadcaster Curt Gowdy, speaking fondly of the longtime Red Sox star, introduced Williams to the crowd. As usual, Williams was honest, if not politically correct in making some of his remarks. "In spite of all the terrible things that have been said about me by the [knights] of the keyboard . . . and they were terrible things—I'd like to forget them but I can't," Williams said into the microphone before pausing momentarily and changing his tone. "I want to say that my years in Boston have been the greatest thing in my life."[14] Williams then went on to praise Tom Yawkey as the greatest owner in the game and the Boston fans as the finest in the land. While Yawkey and many of the fans in attendance probably appreciated Ted's sentiment, the writers in attendance bristled at his latest swipe at the media.

Williams' major league swan song would take place against the Orioles, who were starting a young left-hander named Steve Barber. "I went into that game thinking, 'Gee this is the last game for me.' We were playing Baltimore and Barber, a little pitcher for Baltimore. A tough little pitcher too, he was a good little pitcher, but he was wild that day. He walked me that first time up, he didn't even get through the lineup and they got him out of there; he was walking everybody."[15] Barber failed to register even a single out, giving way to veteran reliever Jack Fisher.

After Williams walked on four pitches in his first at-bat against Barber, he managed to put the ball in play against Fisher, but with little success. Williams flied out to center field, and then flied out deep to right field; the second ball initially appeared to have home run distance, but didn't carry on the cold, damp day while also being affected by an east wind.[16] Baltimore's Al Pilarcik caught it right in front of the 380-foot sign. "If that one didn't go out, none of them will today,"[17] Williams told power-hitting teammate Vic Wertz, recognizing that the heaviness of the air would make it nearly impossible to reach the seats.

In the eighth inning, Williams took what everyone realized would be his final at-bat at Fenway. Williams again faced Fisher, the veteran right-hander. Fisher delivered the first pitch wide of the strike zone, with the ever-patient Williams allowing it to pass for ball one. Now down in the count, Fisher elected to throw a fastball. Williams swung, but completely missed the pitch, late with his offering. Williams felt he should have hammered the pitch, which only added to his frustration on the unpleasant day.

Figuring that he had thrown one fastball past the aging Williams, Fisher decided to try another. With the count now 1-and-1, Williams now had his second chance. Summoning extra strength on the cold and bitter day, Williams swung hard, connected hard, and powered the waist-high, outside-corner fastball 450 feet toward the right-center field bleachers at Fenway Park. The long line drive, traveling on a low trajectory, missed the bleachers because of its lack of height, instead landing on the canopy above the bullpen bench. After bouncing off the canopy, the ball rattled up against the wire fence that blocked off the front row of the bleachers, and then bounced back into the bullpen.[18] Williams' 29th home run of the season, a storybook blast, prompted thousands of amazed Red Sox fans to give him a standing ovation.

Circling the bases, Williams ran with his head down—something that he always did after hitting home runs—not allowing a smile to cross his face.[19] As Williams prepared to touch home plate, he shook hands with young Red Sox catcher Jim Pagliaroni (who had idolized Ted, prompting him to sign with the organization), still maintaining his head in a downward position. When Williams approached the dugout, many of the fans in the crowd began to roar more loudly, hoping they could convince Ted to take a bow and tip his cap. Williams considered the possibility, but remembered what he had promised himself long ago. He had vowed to himself that he would never doff his cap after the harsh treatment he had endured earlier in his career. He refused to tip his cap, not even at such an emotional moment, with such persistent prompting of the fans, who chanted "We want Ted!" for several minutes. "I just couldn't do it," Williams said later. "It just would not have been me."[20] Several Red Sox players, and even some of the umpires, pleaded with Ted to step out onto the field and tip his cap to the fans, but he remained stubborn in his wish to stay in the dugout. As John Updike wrote in the *New Yorker*, "Gods do not answer letters."[21]

In later years, Williams offered a more in-depth review of his refusal to tip his cap, contrasting it with his reaction to fans during his first major league season. "I used to tip my hat," Williams explained. "I used to give it the biggest tip in baseball. Right from the button. I was so enthusiastic in those days [his rookie season]. But no more. They soured me [by booing me]. I made up mind a long time ago that I'd never tip my hat. And I won't."[22]

Although Williams clearly did not tip his cap after hitting his final home run, that fact did not prevent some media outlets from reporting otherwise. The next day, Yankee broadcaster Phil Rizzuto made mention of Williams' home run on New York's telecast, while emphasizing the point that Ted had tipped his cap. In the first issue of the *Sporting News* that hit newsstands after Williams' swan song, the headline over the Red Sox beat column declared: SPLINTER TIPS CAP TO HUB FANS AFTER FAREWELL HOMER. As with many baseball legends, such accounts made the story a bit more dramatic, but that much further from the truth.

Casting aside his refusal to tip his cap, those in attendance continued to applaud in amazement over Williams' tour de force in his final at-bat. Williams surprised even himself with his show of power at such a climactic time. "I didn't have any ideas about home runs; I just tried to hit the ball hard," Williams told the Hall of Fame.

> To show you how and why I consider myself the luckiest guy that ever hit, I had hunches and I could guess good and one of them was the last time at bat. I'd hit two balls damn good that day and I thought they were going to go, but they didn't. So, here I am my last time at-bat, two runs behind, nobody on. He laid a ball right there, I don't think I ever missed like I missed that one, but I missed that one. It's the first time in my life I said, "Oh geez, what happened, why didn't I hit that one?" I couldn't believe it, it was great, not the fastest pitch I'd ever seen, good stuff. I missed the swing and . . . I didn't know what to think. . . . Was I ahead or was I behind? It was . . . right in a [good spot] to hit and I swung, had a hell of a swing and I missed it. I'm still there trying to figure out, what the hell happened. I could see Fisher out there.[23]

As Ted observed Fisher, something about his body language tipped off the identity of the next pitch, which would be the same as the last one.

> And I saw that and I guess it woke me up, you know. Right away I assumed, he thinks he threw it by me. You know, give me the ball quick, right away I said, I know he's going to go right back with that pitch and sure enough here it goes. I hit that one just a little better then I did the other two. And I got it. . . . There's the lucky part right there. He gave the pitch away practically; he gave it away. I assumed [the pitch] just by his actions and I was right and I must have given it a little extra something because that one there did go.[24]

It went, and the home run proved crucial in the Red Sox 5–4 victory over the Orioles.

Even in later years, Ted remained humble about his final at-bat, crediting chance more than his own ability. "Well, you got to be lucky," Williams said sincerely. "I'm going to tell you there's guys that I know that had as much ability [as me] and maybe more. I know some that had more ability than I had."[25] Yet, very few had succeeded in ending their careers so theatrically—and appropriately.

There was something else appropriate about Williams and his final total of home runs. For Williams it was his 521st career home run, placing him firmly in third place on the all-time list. He had finished behind only Babe Ruth and Jimmie Foxx, both former Red Sox greats.

At the start of the ninth inning, manager Pinky Higgins sent Williams out to left field. As Williams ran toward his position, backup outfielder Carroll Hardy followed just a few feet behind—at Higgins' instruction. When Hardy arrived in left field to take Ted's place, Williams began his retreat toward the dugout. Higgins wanted to give Williams one final chance to run off the field, a final opportunity to receive thanks from those in attendance at Fenway Park, and perhaps most importantly, one last chance to tip his cap to the fans. As Williams jogged from left field to the Red Sox dugout, he received another standing ovation. Yet, Williams still would not tip his cap, as tempting as it might have been.

After the game, sportswriter Ed Linn approached Williams and asked him if he had given any thought to presenting the fans with a "show of good feeling."[26] Williams responded quickly and curtly. "I felt nothing."[27] Linn tried to follow up by asking Ted if he had felt any sense of sentimentality or gratitude, or even sadness. "I said *nothing*," Williams replied with emphasis. "Nothing, nothing, nothing!"[28]

Regardless of his true feelings toward the fans, Williams had amassed one of the most impressive resumes of baseball's modern era, capping it off with a theatrical finale. After he sat out the season-ending road trip to New York—a plan that was revealed to the public in the hours after his Fenway finale—the numbers of his final season looked like those belonging to a player in his prime, not one who was seeking retirement. A .316 batting average and 29 home runs indicated that Williams still had vast hitting ability left at the age of 42.

Still, Williams had decided that nineteen seasons in a Red Sox uniform was sufficient. He finished his career with two MVP awards, six batting titles, and four American League home run and RBI crowns apiece. He accumulated eight seasons in which he blasted 30 or more home runs and eleven seasons in which he drew 100 or more walks. At the time of his retirement, Williams placed in the top ten all-time of several major categories: third all-time in home runs; sixth in RBIs, eighth in runs, eighth in total bases, second in walks (to Babe Ruth), and fifth in batting average. More importantly, he had succeeded in making himself the most popular player in the history of one of baseball's oldest franchises. As biographer Ed Linn wrote: "And now Boston knows how England felt when it lost India."[29]

Not everyone appreciated Williams' contributions as a player. Sportswriter Huck Finnegan, writing for the *Boston American* on the very day that Williams played his final game, emphasized the star's failures: "Williams' career, in contrast [to Babe Ruth's], has been a series of failures except for his averages. He flopped in the only World Series he ever played in [in 1946] when he batted only .200. He flopped in the playoff game with Cleveland in 1948. He flopped in the final game of the 1949 season with the pennant hinging on the outcome. He flopped in 1950 when he returned to the lineup after a two-month absence and ruined the morale of a club that seemed pennant-bound under [manager] Steve O'Neill. It has always been Williams' records first, the team second, and the Sox non-winning record is proof of that."[30]

While some of Finnegan's individual points contained merit, they collectively added up to a one-sided and picayune critique of a man whose personality had clashed with too many Boston sportswriters. It hardly seemed fair—or accurate—to heap all of the blame for the Red Sox many failures on the man who had been their best player for over twenty seasons.

In fact, according to many Sabermetricians who have studied Williams' career it was more than unfair or misleading—it was a downright twisted distortion of the truth. As the game's most dominant hitter for the better part of two decades, Williams seemed to deserve far more credit for the Red Sox few team successes than he merited any significant share of blame for the franchise's many disappointments. If a few more hitters and several more pitchers on the Red Sox had come close to displaying some of the greatness of Ted Williams, it would have been Boston challenging New York for baseball supremacy throughout the 1940s and 1950s. That's not to say that Williams didn't have his flaws as a player—he didn't work hard enough on his defensive play and was never a skilled baserunner—but the flaws of Boston's supporting cast had far more to do with Red Sox shortfalls than anything Ted Williams failed to do from the last year of the 1930s through the first year of the 1960s.

NOTES

1. Shaughnessy, "The Kid," 77.
2. Ibid.
3. Williams, with Pietrusza, *Teddy Ballgame*, 135.
4. Linn, "The Kid's Last Game," 52–63.
5. Ibid.
6. Ibid.
7. Ibid.
8. Ibid.
9. Interview with Ted Williams, conducted by Jeff Idelson of the National Baseball Hall of Fame, 2000.
10. Ibid.
11. Linn, "The Kid's Last Game," 52–63.
12. Ibid.
13. Ibid.

14. Updike, "Hub Fans Bid Kid Adieu," 109–110.

15. Interview with Ted Williams, conducted by Jeff Idelson of the National Baseball Hall of Fame, 2000.

16. Updike, "Hub Fans Bid Kid Adieu," 109–110.

17. Smith, *Storied Stadiums*, 174.

18. Linn, "Growing Up With Ted," 56.

19. Pietrusza et al., *Baseball*, 1237.

20. Chadwick and Spindel, *The Boston Red Sox*, 81.

21. Updike, "Hub Fans Bid Kid Adieu," 109–110.

22. Linn, "Growing Up With Ted," 79.

23. Interview with Ted Williams, conducted by Jeff Idelson of the National Baseball Hall of Fame, 2000.

24. Ibid.

25. Ibid.

26. Linn, "Growing Up With Ted," 56.

27. Ibid.

28. Ibid.

29. Linn, "The Kid's Last Game," 56.

30. Huck Finnegan, *Boston American*, September 28, 1960.

BEYOND THE BALLFIELD

The end of his Red Sox season in 1960 did not end Williams' commitment to baseball that fall. He immediately reported to Pittsburgh for the start of the World Series, as part of his commitment to follow the Fall Classic for *Life* magazine. Williams filed reports on what became a most memorable Series, with the rival Yankees losing to the underdog Pirates on Bill Mazeroski's indelible home run in Game 7.

The winter brought Ted some much-needed rest before his next assignment, which was scheduled to begin in the spring. Having agreed to remain with the Red Sox organization as a part-time hitting instructor, Williams reported to the team's spring site in Scottsdale, Arizona. The commitment to the Red Sox would encompass only the duration of spring training, leaving Ted free to spend his time as he pleased during the regular season.

With his retirement official and his playing days in the past, Williams soon received an intriguing, but little-known offer from another team. No media sources reported the story at the time, and Williams only revealed details of the offer in his later years. The offer came in 1961 from the Red Sox chief rivals, the New York Yankees, who wanted Williams to serve as a kind of pinch-hitter extraordinaire.[1] Williams wouldn't start games—the designated hitter rule was still more than a decade away—and wouldn't have to play the field; he would simply be available to pinch-hit in the late innings of games. For that, he would receive a salary of $125,000.[2]

To accept the offer from the hated Yankees, Williams would have to receive permission from the Red Sox, who still owned his rights. That wasn't likely to

On July 25, 1966, during one of the most memorable induction ceremonies that Coopers-town, New York, has ever experienced, Williams makes a heartfelt plea for stars of the Negro Leagues to receive the rewards of Hall of Fame election. *National Baseball Hall of Fame Library, Cooperstown, N.Y.*

happen, given the bitter feelings that annually persisted between the two organizations. As it turned out, the Red Sox feelings on the matter never became an issue. Williams considered the offer from the Yankees, but turned it down. Already worn down by age and injuries, he regarded New York City and its surrounding areas as too hectic and frenetic.

Another factor might have affected Ted's thinking about extending his career with the Yankees. He didn't really enjoy playing in Yankee Stadium, despite the constant speculation by fans and media that he would have thrived playing his entire career in a ballpark that favored left-handed pull hitters. After his playing days, Williams discussed the specific difficulties of hitting in Yankee Stadium: "There's the bigness of it. There are those high stands and all those people smoking—and, of course, the shadows. . . . It takes at least one series to get accustomed to the Stadium and even then you're lost."[3]

For Williams, feeling "lost" apparently created a different set of results than for most other players. Williams managed to compile a more-than-respectable batting average of .309 in over 450 career at-bats at Yankee Stadium, belying some of his complaints about having to hit in the "House That Ruth Built." Still, Williams maintained, even in his later years, that the Stadium created problems because of the way that pitchers kept the ball away from him. "I always thought Yankee Stadium was the toughest place to hit because they always said, 'Don't let him beat you,' and they always said, 'Don't let him pull you,'" Williams told the Hall of Fame. "If you walk [me], what's the difference, he's [just at] first base and you have a double play all set up."[4]

In contrast to Yankee Stadium, Williams truly enjoyed playing in Fenway Park. Much cozier than the big ballyard in the Bronx, Fenway Park provided Williams with a feeling of comfort. Though he rarely hit to the opposite field, the proximity of the "Green Monster" in left field gave Fenway a certain intimacy preferred by hitters. The ballpark also supplied an excellent background for batters, with no advertising on the outfield walls, something that Williams considered important in the scheme of hitting. In addition, there was little foul territory, which meant that most foul pop-ups would stray into the stands, giving a hitter a chance to prolong his at-bat. Not surprisingly, Williams performed exceptionally well at Fenway. He batted .361 lifetime in Boston, compared to .328 on the road. In each of three particularly remarkable seasons (1941, 1951, and 1957), he bettered the .400 mark at Fenway. He also hit with enormous power at home, often reaching such tape-measure dimensions with his home runs that the long distance to right and right center field simply didn't matter. A specially designated red seat at Fenway shows where a 502-foot blast by Williams once landed; it's still regarded as the longest home run in the history of Boston's grand old park.

Now fully resolved to the end of his playing days, Ted opted to leave the mainstream of organized baseball. Rather than accept a fulltime coaching position or a minor league managing post, both of which would have been within easy reach, Williams decided to work only as a spring training instructor and instead devoted most of his efforts toward baseball at the youth level. He opened up a baseball camp for boys from the ages of 8 to 19 in Lakeville, Massachusetts.[5] Recalling his own experiences as a youngster in a YMCA camp, Williams decided to spend some of his spare time working with young players on improving their baseball skills, in particular their abilities with the bat. The camp also figured to keep Williams out of the media spotlight that would have accompanied any kind of extended on-field position in professional baseball.

With his full-time major league affiliations now ended, Ted decided to abandon his single lifestyle and pursue marriage for a second time. In 1961, he wed Lee Howard,[6] a Chicago-area socialite whom he had first met late in his major league career. Williams figured that his second attempt at marriage would prove far better than his first, what with the rigors and travel of the long baseball season no longer running interference. Unfortunately, a respite from major league baseball didn't help Williams' home life. He and Lee frequently argued, with the couple quickly seeking divorce.[7] Much to his disappointment, Williams' second marriage failed to come close to matching his ten-year union with his first wife, Doris.

Ted Williams first became eligible for election to the Hall of Fame in 1966, after the mandatory five-year waiting period required by the Hall's rules for election. Not surprisingly, Williams received considerable support from the Baseball Writers' Association of America. Williams was named on an overwhelming 93.38 percent of the ballots cast (282 of 302), well beyond the 75 percent required for election to the Cooperstown shrine. For Williams, it was a great honor, but one that he had managed to avoid obsessing about during his career. "Oh, I never really thought of that too much," Williams told the Hall of Fame in an interview during the year 2000. "I was making baseball history, but I never thought of the Hall of Fame. All I wanted was [for] guys to see me going down the street and say, 'Boy, that guy was some hitter; he's the best hitter that I ever saw.' I was thinking in terms of that [and] I was creating some [impressive] stats. But I didn't even think of about the stats. About the Hall of Fame and all that. Sure I wanted to lead the league and sure I wanted to hit 35 home runs [each year] and sure I wanted to hit well if I could, but it don't happen all the time."[8]

Williams' induction into the Hall of Fame occurred on July 25, 1966. On a sunny day in Cooperstown, New York, Williams and managerial legend Casey Stengel accepted their plaques and officially joined the ranks of the Hall of Fame.

Both men made memorable speeches in Cooperstown, shortly after being introduced by baseball commissioner William "Spike" Eckert.

"Now ladies and gentlemen," said Eckert, "comes the most important and pleasant part of my role. I am about to induct the two newest members into the Hall of Fame. There was never any doubt that Ted Williams would be elected to the Hall of Fame just as soon as he became eligible. He is the last major leaguer to hit .400. His 521 home runs place him fourth on the all-time list." As Eckert began his next sentence, the fans who had gathered on Main Street intervened with a round of applause. "There are many who insist Ted Williams ranks with Babe Ruth and Ty Cobb as the greatest hitters who ever lived," prompting even louder applause from the crowd. "While Ted's lifetime figures are topped by only a few, there is no telling to what heights those figures would have reached had he not given nearly five full years of his baseball life to the service of his country," prompting more applause. "I think it is safe to assume that Ted would have hit at least a hundred and fifty more home runs and added at least uh, another 500 batted in." At that prompting, one of the fans shouted "250!" inspiring a chuckle from Eckert and laughter from the audience. "Two-fifty," Eckert said in agreement. "It is no wonder that the Baseball Writers' Association of America elected him to the Hall of Fame in one of the greatest landslide votes ever. Ah, Ted, if you will step up here I will read the inscription on the plaque."[9] At that moment, the crowd erupted, forcing Eckert to pause.

"I'll read the plaque," said Eckert. "Theodore Samuel 'Ted' Williams. Boston Red Sox, American League 1939 to 1960. Batted .406 in 1941, led American League in batting six times, slugging percentage nine times, total bases six times, runs scored six times, bases on balls eight times, total hits 2,654, included 521 home runs, lifetime batting average .344, lifetime slugging average .634, Most Valuable American League player in 1946 and 1949, played in eighteen All Star games, named player of the decade, 1951 to 1960. Ted, it is an honor to present you with your eventful . . ."[10] Eckert could not complete his sentence, drowned out by a rapid burst of applause for Williams. As Ted held the plaque, several members of the audience called for him to hold it higher.

Williams read the speech he had written the night before in his Cooperstown hotel room.

> Mr. Commissioner, baseball dignitaries and fans, I'm happy and I want to emphasize what a great honor it is to have the new Commissioner of Baseball here, General Eckert. The General and I have at least one thing in common, we each did some flying. He was in the Air Force and I was a Marine, and I want you to know that no

matter what you might have heard there were many times when the Air Force went out first and the Marines had to go out and hit the targets they missed.[11]

After a short burst of laughter, Williams continued his speech.

I'm sure that every player thinks about someday going into the Hall of Fame. And now that the great moment has come for me, I find it difficult to say what is really in my heart. But I know that it's the greatest thrill of my life. I received 280-odd votes from the writers, and I know that I didn't have 280-odd close friends among the writers."[12]

The crowd laughed again and Williams himself chuckled.

I know they voted for me because they felt in their minds and some in their hearts that I rated it. And I want to say to them, from the heart, thank you. Thank you all from the bottom of my heart (resulting in applause from the crowd).

Today, I'm thinking of a lot of things. I'm thinking of my old playground director in San Diego, California, Rodney Luscomb. My old high school coach, Wos Caldwell. My managers who had such patience with me and helped me so much. Fellows like Frank Shellenback, my first manager in San Diego in 1936; Donie Bush was my manager after the Red Sox bought me and farmed me out to Minneapolis. Joe Cronin, who I can't say enough wonderful things about, and he knows and I know how important he was to me, and Joe McCarthy, one of the greatest managers that ever lived.

I'm thinking today of Eddie Collins, who had such faith in me. You came out in California in 1936. And to be in the Hall of Fame with him particularly, as well as all those other ballplayers is a great honor, and I'm awfully sorry today that Eddie isn't here. I'm thinking of Tom Yawkey. I've always said it, and I'd like to repeat it again today, that to me Tom Yawkey's the greatest owner in baseball, and I was lucky to have played on the club he owned, and I'm grateful here, for his being here today.

But I'm not, [I'd] not be leveling if I left it at that, because ballplayers are not born great, they're not born hitters or pitchers, or managers, and luck isn't the key factor. No one has come up with a substitute for hard work. I've never met a great baseball player who didn't have to work harder at learning to play baseball than anything else he ever did. To me it was the greatest fun I ever had, which probably explains why today I feel both humility and pride, because God let me play the game, and to learn to be good at it. Proud because I spent most of my life in the company of so many wonderful people.

The other day Willie Mays hit his 522nd home run. He has gone past me and he is pushing ahead, and all I can say to him is, 'Go get them, Willie.' Inside this building are plaques to baseball men of all generations, and I'm privileged to join them. Baseball gives every American boy a chance to excel, not just to be as good as someone else, but to be better than someone else. This is the nature of man, and the name of the game, and I've always been a very lucky guy to have worn a baseball uniform. To have struck out, or hit a tape measure home run. And I hope that someday, the names of Satchel Paige and Josh Gibson in some way can be added as a symbol of the Negro players that are not here only because they were not given a chance.[13]

As Williams began to formulate his next sentence, the crowd that had gathered on Cooperstown's Main Street applauded his remarks, which had not been expected or predicted. Williams continued:

As time goes on I'll be thinking baseball, teaching baseball, and arguing for baseball, to keep it right on top of American sports. Just like it is in Japan, and Mexico, Venezuela, and other Latin and South American countries. Now I know Casey Stengel feels the same way, and I'm glad, and I'm awfully glad to be with him on his big day. I also know I'll lose a dear friend if I don't stop talking, as I know I'm eating into his time (drawing laughter from the crowd), and uh, that is, and that is unforgivable. So in closing, I'm grateful, and I know how lucky I was to have been born in America, and had a chance to play the game I loved, the greatest game of them all, baseball.[14]

At the conclusion of Williams' speech, the assembled crowd rewarded him with a prolonged ovation.

On a day in which Williams could have been excused for focusing on his own career accomplishments, he had made a far more noteworthy impression by forwarding the cause of others: calling for the election of former Negro Leagues stars to the Hall of Fame. Five years later, in one of the Hall of Fame's watershed moments, Satchel Paige would become the first Negro Leagues standout to take his place in Cooperstown; for his willingness to speak out, and his direct effect on Hall of Fame rules and policy, Williams was deservedly hailed as a racial pioneer. When Pumpsie Green learned of what Williams had said in favor of the Negro Leagues players at the induction ceremony, he smiled—with good reason.[15]

Williams' visit to Cooperstown not only included the front steps of the Museum, where he delivered his memorable induction speech, but another landmark within the small village. Williams later stopped by Cooperstown's Doubleday Field, located less than two blocks away from the Hall of Fame and Museum. Williams had visited Doubleday Field on several occasions earlier in his career, when he was still an active player for the Red Sox. In 1940, the Red Sox had played the Chicago Cubs in the first annual Hall of Fame Game at Doubleday Field. Williams remembered vividly details of his first game—both the good and the bad—at the tiny, old-fashioned ballpark.

> It was a small ballpark and the most memorable thing I remember in that game . . . [was that] I did hit a home run that day. I didn't hit it good, but it went anyway. The thing that I also remember was that Dominic DiMaggio was on our team that year. He was playing center field; he was a great center fielder. And there was a ball hit in the second inning into right center. There were [temporary] seats out there, the kind you could take down and set them up again. The seats were maybe three feet high. And Dominic was over there and the ball was hit there and [he] ran right into the bleachers and knocked himself down. I thought he was going to kill himself on that play. Well, he was all right but he scared everybody in the ballpark with that job. And, oh, I could never forget that.[16]

Following his memorable Hall of Fame induction, Williams remained out of full-time organized baseball for the next two-and-a-half years. With more free time on his hands, Williams spent an increased amount of time devoting his efforts to his favorite non-baseball pursuit—fishing. Living in Florida, Williams spent much of his time pursuing his hobby. Three kinds of fish interested Williams in particular: bonefish, tarpon, and Atlantic salmon. Williams cited his love of bonefish, a tough game fish, as the primary reason he had moved to the Florida Keys. According to Williams, he had once caught nearly seventy bonefish in 1947, during his first year in the Keys.[17]

Williams' interest in other kinds of fish motivated him to travel. In addition to finding tarpon (a prehistoric fish) near his home in Florida, Williams embarked on tarpon expeditions in the Gulf of Mexico, Texas, and as far away as Costa Rica.[18]

More than tarpon and bonefish, Williams regarded Atlantic salmon as the greatest of all fish. Williams targeted the Miramichi River in New Brunswick as his favored location for Atlantic salmon. At the end of the baseball season, Williams typically traveled to the Miramichi in pursuit of his preferred fish.[19]

Now that he was retired from playing, Williams would make more frequent visits to the Northeast in search of Atlantic salmon. So accomplished in his fishing efforts, Williams would eventually win election to the National Freshwater Fishing Hall of Fame, making him the first man to be inducted in both that shrine and the Baseball Hall of Fame. Williams' collection of Hall of Fame memberships, however, would not end with those two. Over the course of his lifetime, Williams would gain election to a host of halls of fame: two other fishing halls, the Atlantic Salmon Hall of Fame and the International Game Fish Association Hall of Fame; one other baseball shrine, the Hispanic Heritage Baseball Museum Hall of Fame (he became that Hall's first inductee); a military hall, the United States Marine Corps Sports Hall of Fame; and two geographically based shrines, the Florida Sports Hall of Fame and the San Diego Hall of Champions.[20] Yet, a humble Williams always resisted efforts by others to enshrine him in the hall of fame in his own building—the Hitters Hall of Fame at the Ted Williams Museum, located in Hernando, Florida.

With organized baseball mostly out of the picture, Williams also concentrated his efforts on raising a family. In 1968, his first son was born, the product of the marriage to his third wife, Dolores Wettach,[21] a model for *Vogue* magazine and a onetime Miss Vermont who had been a contestant in a Miss Universe pageant. Ted settled on the name John Henry for the newborn boy, believing that such a name conveyed strength and fortitude, traits that Williams admired. The Williams family would continue to expand, with the birth of a daughter, named Claudia, the following year. Unfortunately, the arrival of children did not solve Ted's failed pursuits of wedded bliss. Ted's relationship with Dolores would last longer than his marriage to Lee Howard, but far shorter than his initial wedlock with Doris Soule, ultimately enduring the same fate as his first two marriages—an unpleasant divorce.[22]

Williams also took some time to work on a book about his life, in particular his career in baseball. Collaborating with acclaimed Miami-based writer John Underwood, Williams produced a book titled *My Turn at Bat: The Story of My Life*. The book, published in 1969, received critical acclaim, including a favorable review from the *New York Times*.[23]

In the meantime, reporters repeatedly sought out Williams' opinion about present-day hitters, especially young hitters who had burst onto the scene with impressive displays of high-average hitting. One such young player was the Pittsburgh Pirates' Matty Alou, previously a poor hitter with the San Francisco Giants who suddenly emerged as a star in 1966. The unorthodox batting approach of the pesky Alou—swinging at pitches out of the strike zone, refusing to take walks, and insistence on hitting off of his front foot while using a remarkably heavy bat—represented the diametrical opposite of Williams' fundamental approach to hitting. Alou strode with his right foot first, kept his bat back as long as possible, and then flicked his wrists, often blooping balls into short left field for base hits. "He violates every hitting principle I ever taught," Williams told the *Sporting News* when asked to critique Alou's style at the plate.[24] Yet, by bunting frequently, chopping down on the ball in an effort to beat out infield singles, and spraying the ball from foul line to foul line, Alou won the National League batting title with a .342 average in 1966, and bettered the .330 mark each of the next three seasons. It certainly wouldn't have worked for Williams—and most hitters for that matter—but it paid dividends for the diminutive, five-foot, nine-inch Alou.

Occasional interviews with the media, publishing efforts, spring training work as a batting instructor, a lucrative contract to serve as a spokesman for Sears-Roebuck, and occasional devotion to his growing family all occupied Williams' time during his post-playing hiatus of the 1960s. Given all of his commitments, it may have seemed like Williams enjoyed a busy and fulfilling agenda as part of his "second" career. Yet, in the minds of a growing number of people connected with baseball, something was missing. Two people, in particular, set out to change Ted's career path by reintroducing him to the game that had once consumed his day-to-day life.

NOTES

1. Williams, with Pietrusza, *Teddy Ballgame*, 136.
2. Dan Shaughnessy, "Ted Williams: A Life Remembered—Plenty on His Plate," *Boston Globe*, July 6, 2002, online edition.
3. Riley, *The Red Sox Reader*, 61.
4. Interview with Ted Williams, conducted by Jeff Idelson of the National Baseball Hall of Fame, 2000.
5. Williams, with Pietrusza, *Teddy Ballgame*, 154.
6. Davis, *The Scribner Encyclopedia of American Lives*, 503.
7. Ibid.
8. Interview with Ted Williams, conducted by Jeff Idelson of the National Baseball Hall of Fame, 2000.
9. Hall of Fame Induction Transcript, 1966.
10. Ibid.
11. Ibid.
12. Ibid.
13. Ibid.
14. Ibid.
15. Bryant, *Shut Out*, 66.

16. Interview with Ted Williams, conducted by Jeff Idelson of the National Baseball Hall of Fame, 2000.

17. Williams, with Pietrusza, *Teddy Ballgame*, 149.

18. Ibid.

19. Ibid.

20. Nowlin and Prime, *The Pursuit of Perfection: Ted Williams*, 247.

21. Davis, *The Scribner Encyclopedia of American Lives*, 503.

22. Ibid.

23. Williams, with Pietrusza, *Teddy Ballgame*, 154.

24. Charley Feeney, *Sporting News*, date unknown.

Forging a new legacy as a manager, Williams combines his two great loves; a uniformed Williams tinkers with a fishing reel during the Washington Senators spring training camp in Pompano Beach, Florida. *Photo courtesy of Bruce Markusen.*

THE MANAGERIAL CHAIR

Other than his spring training work with the Red Sox and his 1966 induction to the Hall of Fame, Williams had become somewhat disassociated from the National Pastime. He no longer worked in the game on a full-time basis, and was becoming better known to younger fans as the commercial pitchman for Sears-Roebuck, in much the same way that the newer generation related to former New York Yankees great Joe DiMaggio as "Mr. Coffee."

Ted's continued absence from the game likely would have lasted even longer if not for a surprising phone call he received from Bob Short, the new owner of the Washington Senators. In taking over the operation of the Senators, perennially one of the worst teams in the American League, Short hoped to turn the franchise around—fast. As part of his plan, he wanted to make major headlines by hiring one of baseball's biggest names to serve as his field manager. Acting quickly, Short placed a long-distance phone call to Williams at his home in the Florida Keys.

Short told Williams that he wanted to replace Jim Lemon, the Senators' current manager. He wanted to fill the managerial vacancy with Williams, who had never managed at any level. Williams, who had reportedly turned down an offer to become Red Sox manager several years earlier, replied that he knew almost nothing about the intricacies of managing and knew little about the Senators' personnel, other than star outfielder Frank Howard and a few other players. In summary, Williams told Short no, that he still wasn't interested in managing and that the owner should pursue someone else to fill the position.[1] Ted thought that his immediate and definitive reply would halt Short's interest in him, but it didn't.

Short called Williams again, only to be rejected a second time. Still, Short didn't give up. He asked American League president Joe Cronin to intercede, to plead his case with Williams. He hoped that Cronin's past association as Ted's manager in Boston would help him exert some influence on Williams' decision. Cronin asked Williams to accept the offer to become the Senators' new manager, in part because it would be good for the American League in particular and for baseball in general.[2]

After Cronin did his best to convince Williams, Short called again. The two men agreed to meet at the Marriott Hotel in Atlanta, where they had dinner together and talked for several hours. Short made a good impression on Williams, swaying him with his smarts and initiative. Williams, an avid member of the Republican Party who had made major financial contributions to the GOP, didn't seem bothered that Short had worked as treasurer of the Democratic Party. He was willing to keep an open mind about Short.

Short's enthusiasm and persistence, along with Cronin's earlier conversations and a generous offer of a $1.25 million contract and stock options to purchase ten percent of the team,[3] combined to forge an influence on Williams. There were other factors at work, as well. As much as Williams loved to hunt and fish, those endeavors could only occupy so much time and challenge him only so much. In addition, Williams' part-time job as a spring training instructor for the Red Sox over the last eight years had become increasingly less satisfying to him. "This may be my last real chance to get back into baseball on my own terms," Williams told John Underwood of *Sports Illustrated*.[4] Ted wanted to teach baseball and hitting on a full-time basis,[5] not just during the spring. After careful consideration and internal debate, Williams decided to take up employment as the new manager of the Washington Senators.

The deal between Williams and Washington became public on January 18, 1969, when the Senators announced the hiring of the most famous manager in the short history of a team that had begun as an expansion franchise in 1961 (the original franchise by the same name moved to become the Minnesota Twins the same year). The Senators, the last-place residents of the American League in 1968, announced that Williams agreed to a five-year contract worth a reported salary of $75,000 per season. The actual figures of Williams' contract, however, were much higher than that, especially given the inclusion of stock options in the franchise. Short also agreed to give Williams an expensive apartment and unlimited expense account.[6] In addition to managing the Senators, Williams would receive the title of vice president. Perhaps the most intriguing clause to be included in the contract was that Williams could *not* be fired. Williams could quit if he wanted to, with the option of moving up to the front office as the team's general manager or returning to his more leisurely life in the Florida Keys. That would be Williams' choice, not Short's.

The Senators set up Williams' first press conference as manager at Miami International Airport.[7] In contrast to his many difficulties with the media throughout his playing career, Williams handled the press conference with unexpected smoothness. Seemingly enjoying the situation, Ted answered questions freely and even participated in some one-on-one interviews. Showing confidence in his new appointed rounds, Williams offered a public promise to the media and fans. "I guarantee you we will win more games," Williams said convincingly.[8]

Williams made a strong impression on the members of the media who had gathered at the press conference. One television sportscaster expressed amazement at what he considered Ted's newfound charm. "Baloney," Williams said loudly while maintaining a large grin. "That just goes to show how little you know me."[9]

At the press conference, the cheery Williams emphasized that he expected few problems dealing with the Washington media. According to Williams, he had dealt with reporters from Washington during his playing days and had encountered no difficulties. "There was only one little town I had trouble in," Williams quipped, making a reference to the city of Boston.[10] When one of the assembled reporters asked him what he would do on Senators road trips into Boston, Williams supplied some more humor. "Hide in the dugout," Williams said succinctly.[11] Yes, this was a different side to Williams' personality, one that he had resisted showing during most of his playing career with the Red Sox.

Although the Senators already announced the deal that would bring Williams back to baseball, Ted had not yet officially signed his five-year contract with Washington. That would come on February 21, just a few days before the start of spring training. The informal Williams even wore a tie to the event—albeit a Texas-style Bolo tie. Both he and Short smiled widely during the signing ceremony, as photographers closed in on the two new partners. For a man who had previously expressed reservations about managing, Williams seemed very content with his new position in baseball.

Short made Williams the centerpiece to his 1969 Senators theme, which became known by the catch phrase, "It's A Whole New Ballgame." The phrase certainly didn't refer to the Senators' stagnant roster of players, which remained virtually the same as it had been during the lackluster 1969 season. The "new ballgame" might as well have been called "Teddy Ballgame," upon whom Short had predicated most of his hopes for an improved season.

At the start of spring training in Pompano Beach, Florida, Williams made no complaints about the lack of change in the Senators' questionable on-field personnel. In somewhat of a surprising declaration, Williams made it clear that he would oversee both the hitters and the pitchers—not just the hitters—with pitching coach Sid Hudson providing advice and counsel when necessary. Committed to work with the players that Short had given him, Williams laid out a simple but highly ambitious goal for the upcoming season. He wanted each player on the Senators to show some kind of improvement in his game—even if only by a small degree—during the 1969 season. Given the absence of real talent, much of the media covering the Senators felt that Williams had laid out an impossible task for the summer ahead.

More specifically, Williams felt that each one of the Senators' position players (the non-pitchers) was capable of becoming a better hitter. "I haven't seen one player on this team—there's not one guy playing the game—who can't be improved," Williams told reporters after watching his Senators manage only one hard-hit ball (by outfielder Brant Alyea) in the team's first intrasquad game of the spring. "Fifty percent of hitting is from the neck up. Concentration. Learning. Studying. Remembering where every pitch was and what it was. I ask these guys today where the ball was that [Brant] Alyea hit. They didn't know. But maybe now they start to think. To study. To remember. Maybe by the time we start the season, they're in the habit of remembering. That part of hitting is something that can be taught. This is where I can help them."[12]

Williams made every effort to help the Senators hitters while doubling as the team's hitting instructor. He put in long hours during the spring, teaching and preaching to his hitters, offering them advice, boosting their confidence, pleading with them to be patient, telling them to wait before swinging. He even did the same calisthenics as his players,[13] in part to lose some weight but also to set a proper example. He closely observed American League opponents, hoping to learn as much as he could about a league that had almost completely turned over in personnel since his retirement nine years ago.[14] All the while, he dealt with a madhouse of media and fan attention, doing his best to accommodate the scores of writers and autograph seekers who had decided to make Pompano Beach the center of the baseball world.

After a grueling spring, which included eight consecutive losses at the start of the exhibition season, Williams officially made his managerial debut on Opening Day, April 7. As per baseball tradition, the Senators always opened a new baseball season at home, where Robert F. Kennedy (RFK) Stadium provided the setting, with the nation's sitting president usually in attendance for what was unofficially called the "Presidential opener." It was no different on this occasion; a crowd of over 45,000 fans, including President Richard Nixon, packed the stadium. As the President threw out the first pitch from the front row of RFK Stadium, Williams and baseball Commissioner Bowie Kuhn stood side by side, watching the Commander-in-Chief from just a few feet away. President Nixon's presence at Williams' debut seemed especially fitting, because both he and Williams were staunch Republicans.

Unfortunately, the Senators couldn't cap off the eventful day with what Williams desired most—a victory against the rival Yankees. Instead, Williams and the Senators lost the opening game to New York, 8–4. Williams was now 0-and-1 in his new job and facing an expected uphill struggle as the skipper of a doormat franchise.

Throughout the spring and the early days of the regular season, much of the media forecast disastrous results for Williams as a manager. Citing his lack of patience and unwillingness to compromise his beliefs, many writers believed that the independent, unyielding Williams would prove an abject failure in the dugout. Some believed that he would tear his nervous system apart while watching his hitters flail away. Their predictions of doom would turn out to be grossly exaggerated.

Reacting well to the teachings of their new field manager, the Senators opened the season by winning sixteen of their first twenty-seven games. Riding a five-game winning streak on May 6, the Senators embarked on their first West Coast trip of the season. The Senators promptly lost their first two games to the Oakland A's—understandable given Oakland's burgeoning talent base, which included Sal Bando, Bert "Campy" Campaneris, Reggie Jackson, and Jim "Catfish" Hunter. Then came embarrassment. The Senators found themselves swept three straight games by the Seattle Pilots, a lowly American League expansion team. Washington then dropped the first game of a series against the California Angels, extending their losing streak to six games. By the time Washington's road trip ended with a series in Chicago, the Senators had lost nine of twelve games overall, including seven of eight on the West Coast. The painful results sank the Senators below the .500 level.

The lowlight of the road trip occurred on May 10, the middle game of the three-game set against the Pilots. Nursing a comfortable 11–3 lead, the Senators' pitching staff imploded, allowing 13 runs over the second half of the game on the way to a demoralizing 16–13 loss. When asked about the distressing developments of the game, Williams opted not to second-guess himself for any in-game decisions, which included the use of six pitchers. In contrast to other games, where Williams had admitted to leaving a pitcher in for one too many batters,[15] Williams felt he had made solid decisions in changing pitchers this time. "I don't know what I could have done differently," Williams told Washington reporters in assessing the team's embarrassing failure to protect an 8-run lead.[16]

Another losing streak soon followed, this one also involving the Pilots and another expansion team, the Kansas City Royals. The six-game skid, which included a pair of extra-inning losses, revealed Williams' Senators as something other than a legitimate contender. Still, the Senators did not fall apart. They responded by winning three of their last four games in May, and then proceeded to play slightly above .500 in each of the summer months of June, July, and August. The Senators performed even more capably in September, forging winning streaks of four and six games on the way to posting seventeen wins during the final full month of the season.

Williams' approach to managing gained favor with many of the Senators' players. The comments of outfielder Brant Alyea exemplified the positive spirit of Ted's teachings. "I'm just beginning to realize that baseball is at least 65 percent psychological," Alyea said in a 1969 discussion with Jim Bouton, pitcher and author of the critically-acclaimed *Ball Four*. "Williams has these guys so psyched they actually think they're great ballplayers. [Eddie] Brinkman's starting to think he's a hitter for crissakes and he's hit .200 all his life. Now he's up to .280. The team is up, the guys are emotionally high, and Williams actually has them believing they're winners."[17]

In addition to stressing the mental aspect of the game, Williams also tried to change the lifestyle habits of his players. An ardent opponent of both first and second-hand smoke, he encouraged players to stop smoking, which he rightly considered a vice antithetical to the proper conditioning of a ballplayer. He told his players not to play golf during the season, so as not to wear themselves out from the rigors of 18 holes.[18] He even lectured his players about the importance of taking daytime naps, under the theory that a player could reach his physical peak two hours after waking up.[19] Some of Williams' theories might have seemed like old wives' tales, while others conformed to logic; either way, Williams succeeded in placing his own forceful and definitive stamp on the Senators.

With the team's morale bolstered and the club exhibiting timely hitting and improved pitching, Williams felt playful enough to have some fun with the writers covering the Senators. He repeatedly told a story about conversations he had held with several writers during the spring. "I asked the regular writers in spring training who were our best pitchers," Williams said, "and they said Camilo Pascual, Barry Moore, Jim Hannan, and Joe Coleman. So who are our best pitchers?" Williams asked rhetorically before supplying his own answer. "[Dick] Bosman and Casey Cox."[20] Although Williams delivered the assessment good-naturedly, he took pleasure in reminding the writers that they had been wrong.

The final day of the season provided a fitting end to what had been a positive season for Williams and the Senators. As Williams walked the lineup card to home plate for the traditional pregame meeting with umpires, he received a standing ovation from the crowd at RFK Stadium. (Fans in Washington had certainly responded to Williams' presence, as evidenced by the near doubling of the Senators' attendance in 1969 from the previous year.) Williams then watched Joe Coleman, one of the writers' preseason choices, pitch skillfully in earning his twelfth victory of the season, a 3–2 decision over Williams' former team, the Red Sox. Feeling in a particularly good mood after the win, Williams lifted his usual fifteen-minute postgame ban against writers in the clubhouse, a policy that he borrowed from his playing days, when Red Sox management felt that the players needed a "cooling off" period before meeting members of the media. On this, the final day of the season, Williams felt no need for any cooling off.

Williams had good reason for feeling light-hearted. Much to the surprise of the Williams naysayers, the Senators pitching showed promise under his guidance. Two of the aforementioned young hurlers, Dick Bosman and Casey Cox, along with fellow right-hander Joe Coleman, formed the nucleus of a surprisingly dependable starting rotation. Bosman pitched so well that he captured the American League's earned run average (ERA) title.

While a few of the pitchers had stepped up in class, the team's offense showed across-the-board improvement. By the end of the 1969 season, almost every one of the Senators' key players had posted enhanced hitting marks, just as Williams had hoped for in the spring—mostly thanks to the teaching of the manager. Doubling as the team's batting instructor, Williams accomplished his goal of team-wide improvement by stressing the mental aspects of hitting, rather than tinkering with a player's swing or batting stance. "And I did it without changing anybody's hitting style," Williams proclaimed emphatically. "Hitting is from the neck up. That's where I worked on them."[21] Williams preached to his players the importance of taking more pitches and swinging less often at bad pitches, thereby reducing the size of their own personal strike zones. In so doing, Senators hitters performed far better in controlling the strike zone, a skill that had eluded Washington's hitters in recent seasons.

The team's top two sluggers, first baseman Mike Epstein and left fielder Frank "Hondo" Howard, each raised their batting averages and walk totals while cutting down on their strikeouts, with Howard reducing his K's from 141 to 96. At the same time, Howard reached a career high by swatting 48 home runs, while Epstein clubbed 30. Other players like second baseman Bernie Allen, third baseman Ken McMullen, and outfielder Del Unser also enjoyed considerable improvement. Most amazingly, Williams succeeded in turning around the Senators' weakest everyday hitter, light-hitting shortstop Eddie Brinkman. He encouraged Brinkman to choke up on the bat as part of a complete retooling of his approach at the plate. Reducing Brinkman's tendency to uppercut the ball and hit weak pop-ups while convincing him to hit the ball both on the ground and to all fields,[22] Williams helped the shortstop improve his batting average from a shameful .187 in 1968 to a respectable .266 in 1969. That represented a seventy-nine-point improvement, almost unheard of for a veteran major league player.

The cases of individual improvement added up to far better offensive totals for the Senators in 1969. They finished with a respectable .251 team batting average. The Senators walked 630 times, a reflection of their willingness to embrace Williams' philosophy of patience at the plate. By taking more pitches early in the count and forcing pitchers to work from behind, the Senators' hitters also coaxed better pitches later in the count, which resulted in a few more home runs. As a team, the Senators finished the season with 148 home runs, an increase of 24 home runs from 1968.

Bolstered mostly by their improved hitting up and down the lineup, and rejuvenated by a sense of desire and hustle that had eluded past Washington teams, the Senators experienced resurgence as a team. At season's end, the Senators' record stood at a solid 86–76, putting them in fourth place in the American League East division standings. With 21 more wins than they had claimed in 1968, the Senators became the most improved team in the league; after having finished the previous season in last place, the Senators actually staged a temporary battle for third place and finished solidly among the better teams in the American League.

With such a surprising record for a team that had been expected to finish close to the cellar once again, Williams earned yet another individual honor—the American League's Manager of the Year Award. In winning the prestigious award, Williams beat out several illustrious managerial names, including Earl Weaver of the Baltimore Orioles and Billy Martin of the Minnesota Twins, both of whom led their teams to the playoffs. A humble Williams felt that both Martin and Weaver deserved Manager of the Year honors more than himself, but both of those skippers had been equipped with far more talented rosters than Ted's Senators. Neither manager had done as much with as little talent as the man whom some skeptics had predicted would fail badly in his inaugural managerial effort.

NOTES

1. John Underwood, "The Newest Senator in Town," *Sports Illustrated*, February 24, 1969, 20–21.
2. Ibid.
3. Ibid.
4. Ibid.

5. Whitfield, *Kiss It Goodbye*, 44.

6. Ibid.

7. Underwood, "The Newest Senator in Town," 20–21.

8. Ibid.

9. Ibid.

10. Ibid.

11. Ibid.

12. Joe McGinniss, "What Ted Williams Is Like Today," *Sport*, June 1969, 16.

13. Ibid.

14. Ibid.

15. Merrell Whittlesey, "Ted, Nixon, Run Neck-and-Neck in Publicity Glare," *Sporting News*, May 31, 1969, 7.

16. Merrell Whittlesey, *The Sporting News Official Baseball Guide for 1970* (St. Louis: The Sporting News, 1970), 29.

17. Jim Bouton, *Ball Four: The Final Pitch* (Champaign, IL: Sports Publishing, 2000), 158.

18. Whitfield, *Kiss It Goodbye*, 47.

19. Whittlesey, "Ted, Nixon, Run Neck-and-Neck in Publicity Glare," 7.

20. Whittlesey, *The Sporting News Official Baseball Guide for 1970*, 29.

21. Ibid.

22. Merrell Whittlesey, "Ted's Tips Load Brinkman's Bat with Explosive Charge," *Sporting News*, May 24, 1969, 10.

MANAGING THE SOPHOMORE JINX

Heading into his second season at the helm, Williams and the Senators faced the challenge of having to sustain their surprising excellence in 1970. They opened the new year in typical fashion, losing the Presidential opener for the eighth straight season, but otherwise played impressively, winning eleven of nineteen games in April. The Senators also made a prosperous trade with the Angels, sending veteran third baseman Ken McMullen to the California Angels for two younger players of greater promise, fellow third baseman Aurelio Rodriguez and onetime bonus-baby outfielder Rick Reichardt. Rodriguez would emerge as a solid contributor, a premier defensive infielder with burgeoning power at the plate.

At the beginning of May, the Senators lost three straight games before bouncing back with a pair of victories. They seemed to be showing signs of a 1969-type revival. Then, without much warning, the Senators fell back to the reality of the pre-1969 years. They dropped nine consecutive games, including three crushing one-run losses to the lowly Milwaukee Brewers, who had been transplanted to the Midwest after a dismal debut season as the Seattle Pilots. The month of June produced more problems for Washington, including two losing streaks of five games apiece and one stretch of three straight losses.

The season failed to get much better. With too many offensive and pitching deficiencies, Washington finished in last place in the American League East. The Senators struggled against almost every league opponent, losing season series to every team except for the Brewers and White Sox. They also failed to show improvement in the latter stages of the year, losing their last fourteen games in a row, a highly improper sendoff to the season. The disastrous stretch typified a final month of futility for Williams' band. In spite of a productive season that saw him lead the American League in home runs, RBIs, and walks, Frank Howard slumped badly in September. Dick Bosman, who at one time seemed destined to become the Senators' first twenty-game winner, fell short of the milestone by suffering two defeats and a no-decision in his final three starts. In a disappointing follow-up to his league-leading ERA the previous season, Bosman settled for 16 wins in 1970. Bosman also took shots at his teammates for what he perceived as a lack of effort toward the end of the season, but Williams opted not to reprimand his players. Instead, the manager held a more subdued clubhouse meeting at season's end, when he gently suggested that most of the players needed to reapply themselves to the profession of major league baseball.[1]

Two of the Senators' key starting pitchers, Joe Coleman and Casey Cox, regressed after promising 1969 seasons. Another young right-hander, Jim Hannan, lost his last six decisions of the year. Top relief pitcher Darold Knowles, the victim of bad luck and poor run support, lost fourteen games and may have been a victim of overuse by Williams.[2] Offensively, the Senators did little to help their pitchers. The team's batting average fell by thirteen points, while run production dropped off significantly. "Seventy-five fewer runs," Williams moaned. "That's terrible."[3] As a way of addressing the lack of hitting, Bob Short forced Williams to call up the team's top prospect, 19-year-old outfielder Jeff Burroughs. Williams didn't agree with the move; he felt Burroughs wasn't ready for the major leagues. After looking bad in 12 at-bats, the Senators sent Burroughs back to Triple-A Denver and Short admitted to making a mistake. With Burroughs apparently not ready, the Senators lacked a true cleanup hitter, while continuing to struggle with an inability to hit left-handed pitching. (They would finish the season with an unacceptably poor record of fourteen games below .500 against left-handers.) Williams tried to compensate by using frequent platoons of right- and left-handed hitters, but that strategy drew only second-guessing— both from the players and the media.

As much as the Senators' offense struggled, Williams may have placed too much emphasis on working with the team's hitters at the expense of teaching other areas of the game. A humorous incident from the spring illustrated the point. "It's spring training with the Washington Senators, 1970, Pompano Beach, Florida, [and] TW [Ted Williams] is the manager over there working with the outfielders. [Over here] we're going over baserunning. We're going through the rundown [play]," recalled Rick Stelmaszek, a backup catcher with the Senators who later became a coach with the Minnesota Twins. "Joe Camacho, who ran Ted Williams' summer camps in New England, got in an argument over rundowns with Nellie Fox, who played twenty-one seasons in the majors. They get into a heated argument. I mean heated. I thought it was going to come to blows. They're arguing like two little kids. . . . So here comes Big Ted. [He yells] 'WHAT'S UP? WHAT'S UP?' "[4] After each coach made his point about how the rundown should be executed, Williams deliberated momentarily before coming up with a "solution," of sorts. "So Big Ted takes a look at the two of them," said Stelmaszek, "[he] sizes up the situation, and says, 'BLEEP IT! LET'S HIT.' And we never had another fundamental drill that spring."[5] The incident, while both genuinely amusing and emblematic of Williams' obsession with hitting, underscored one of Williams' biggest weaknesses as a manager: an inability to properly emphasize other essential traits of the game as baserunning and defense.

Williams' difficulties with the media, well-chronicled during his playing days, also resurfaced during his second year as the Senators' manager. The frequent second-guessing annoyed Williams greatly, so much so that he feuded with the local writers in the middle of the summer. Williams ended the dispute a few days later when he entered the clubhouse and triumphantly asked of the writers, "Where have you all been?"[6] Still, an underlying tension existed between Williams and the writers throughout the season. Williams' decision to continue to ban writers from the clubhouse for fifteen minutes after each game—which the manager felt would be helpful in serving as a way of letting players wind down after the stress of the game—only aggravated members of the media. As longtime New York scribe Dick Young wrote in describing the fifteen-minute clubhouse ban at season's end, "If it is supposed to be so helpful to the players, how come the Senators finished last?"[7] Yet, Williams indicated that he had no desire to even consider ending the practice of the fifteen-minute ban. "When that goes, I go," said Williams, unwilling to compromise on the matter.[8]

Williams also found himself in conflict with several players, including first baseman Mike Epstein. Sometimes a temperamental sort, Epstein battled with Williams over playing time; Williams liked Epstein, but didn't feel he could hit left-handed pitching well enough to fill an everyday role. "Even in 1969, when I had my best year, I didn't face left-handers," Epstein gasped in an interview with Arnold Hano of *Sport* magazine. "In 1970, the same story. I'd get hot and then they'd throw a left-hander against us, and I'd sit on the bench and cool off. I sat on the bench more and more. It was discouraging."[9] Yet, Williams had made up his mind to use a platoon arrangement, feeling that it provided the best situation for both Epstein and the Senators.

The Senators' many failures convinced Williams that changes needed to be made. He hoped that Bob Short would make some necessary adjustments after the fall to the cellar in 1970. Williams wanted Short to trade Epstein, his top left-handed power hitter. In citing reasons for the team's disappointing finish in

1970, Williams repeatedly pointed to Epstein, who had driven in only fifty-six runs in games in which he had batted cleanup. Although Epstein had shown flashes of stardom for Williams in two seasons with Washington, Ted felt he had reached his peak, was best suited to platoon duty, and would not continue to improve. Williams felt that by trading Epstein, the Senators might be able to acquire a package of players in return, including a solid starting pitcher. That was a commodity that Williams and the Senators needed badly if they hoped to return to the winning ways of 1969.

NOTES

1. Merrell Whittlesey, *The Sporting News Official Baseball Guide for 1971* (St. Louis: The Sporting News, 1971), 37.

2. Whitfield, *Kiss It Goodbye*, 51.

3. Zander Hollander, *The Complete Handbook of Baseball: 1971 Edition* (New York: Lancer Books, 1971), 60.

4. Caple, Jim. "Teddy Ballgame Left His Imprint on Many People," ESPN.com, July 1, 2002, Internet Web site.

5. Ibid.

6. Whittlesey, *The Sporting News Official Baseball Guide for 1971*, 37.

7. Ibid.

8. Hollander, *The Complete Handbook of Baseball*, 67.

9. Arnold Hano, "Mike Epstein: Somewhere Between Journeyman and Superstar," *Sport*, November 1972, 87.

MR. WILLIAMS, MEET
MR. MCLAIN

Bob Short did make a major trade that offseason, but it didn't involve Williams' target, Mike Epstein. Instead, Short made a trade with the Detroit Tigers, a club that was only two years removed from winning a World Championship, but was now willing to surrender the former ace of its pitching staff. In acquiring two-time American League Cy Young winner and former Most Valuable Player Denny McLain, along with three lesser-known players from the Motor City, the Washington owner surrendered slick-fielding shortstop Eddie Brinkman and touted third baseman Aurelio Rodriguez—or what amounted to half of Williams' infield—along with pitchers Joe Coleman and Jim Hannan. In making the trade, Short hoped that McLain could come close to relocating the Cy Young and MVP form that he had displayed in winning thirty-one games for the World Champion Tigers in 1968.

Speaking freely to reporters, Short admitted that Williams did not approve of the deal. The manager had reservations about the trade from the start, partly because of the massive amount of talent that Short had surrendered. Although Williams viewed Coleman as a disappointment because of his inability to emerge as a fifteen-game winner, he regarded Brinkman and Rodriguez quite highly. Williams considered them two of his prized hitting students. He also liked Brinkman's steady fielding at shortstop and the potential that the young Rodriguez possessed with his powerful bat, reliable glove, and cannon-like arm.

Like many others, Williams also harbored concerns over the trade because of McLain's off-the-field troubles. In 1970, Commissioner Bowie Kuhn had suspended McLain for half of the season because of his involvement with illegal

After an exemplary start as manager of the Washington Senators, the toll of overseeing a team of controversial—and limited—talents begins to take its effect on a grimacing Williams. *National Baseball Hall of Fame Library, Cooperstown, N.Y.*

bookmakers and unsavory ties with the gambling world. McLain also received suspensions for carrying a gun and for maliciously treating members of the Detroit press. (He accomplished the latter feat by dumping a bucket of ice water on the heads of two Detroit sportswriters.) In addition, McLain did not pitch well for the Tigers, even after returning to the field once Kuhn's suspension had been lifted.

Williams' worries about McLain were only reaffirmed during the 1971 season; McLain pitched badly for a bad team in Washington. Instead of becoming the Senators' ace, McLain faltered to a miserable record of 10–22, giving him the most losses of any pitcher in the American League. To make matters worse, Williams and McLain found themselves in a severe personality clash. Williams didn't appreciate McLain's unseemly attitude. In turn, McLain didn't like the way that Williams used him as part of the Senators' starting rotation. Williams believed strongly that pitchers should pitch every fifth day, whereas McLain felt more comfortable working out of a four-man rotation. In fact, the controversial right-hander blamed his struggles directly on Williams' insistence that he pitch no more frequently than every fifth day, and sometimes with longer periods of rest. "I threw the ball up until July as well as I ever have for both velocity and strikes," McLain insisted in an interview with Bay Area sportswriter Ron Bergman. "Then Ted Williams said after he had seen me for two months, that it would be better for me to pitch every fifth or sixth day. I thought I was better every fourth day. He had two months of statistics. I had six years of statistics."[1] Reasons and excuses aside, McLain also struggled with the loss of speed on his fastball and the addition of pounds to his waistline. He failed to come up with another pitch to compensate for his lost fastball and continued to pay little attention to his conditioning. McLain's failures on the field and in the clubhouse doomed Williams and the Senators to another losing record in the American League East.

The three other players acquired in the McLain deal also fared miserably: veteran third baseman Don Wert (who never regained effectiveness after a 1968 beaning) started the season in a dreadful 2-for-40 slump and drew his release on June 15; youthful outfielder Elliott Maddox also didn't hit well, finishing at a lowly .217; and pitcher Norm McRae failed to escape the minor leagues. In the meantime, Williams fretted over the loss of the two young infielders that Short had sent to Detroit for McLain. Eddie Brinkman and Aurelio Rodriguez had formed an excellent left side of the infield for the Senators, especially defensively, but now they were long gone, no longer able to help Williams in Washington.

In addition, other veterans besides McLain and Wert failed to pan out for Williams and the Senators. Pitcher Jerry Janeski, a ten-game winner acquired from the White Sox for outfielder Rick Reichardt, flopped badly in Washington. He won only one of ten starts with the Senators, while watching his ERA flutter to nearly 5 runs per game. Third baseman Joe Foy, a onetime member of the Red Sox who had contributed to Boston's "Impossible Dream" pennant chase in 1967, struggled to hit in a Senators uniform. In the middle of June, the Senators demoted Foy to the minors; he never made it back to Washington, drawing his release. And then there was the case of Curt Flood, the challenger to baseball's reserve clause and at one time an All-Star center fielder with the St. Louis Cardinals. Bob Short had coaxed Flood out of retirement, convincing him that he could still play despite missing all of the 1970 season. Beginning the new season in Williams' starting lineup, Flood batted weakly, picking up only 7 singles in 35 April at-bats. Unlike Foy, however, Flood didn't receive his release. Instead, Flood mysteriously abandoned the team on April 27, leaving for Spain on his way to Denmark, and never returning to the Senators' fold.

Simply put, most of Short's off-season acquisitions turned to dust. Even when Short traded away a player that Williams no longer wanted, the deal still backfired. Such was the case when Short finally peddled Mike Epstein, along with ace relief pitcher Darold Knowles, in mid-season, to the Oakland A's for catcher Frank Fernandez, first baseman Don Mincher, pitcher Paul Lindblad, and cash. As much as Williams wanted Epstein out of Washington pinstripes, he probably didn't want him removed at this price. After all, Mincher was older than Epstein—a switch that made little sense for a rebuilding team—Lindblad was arguably an inferior reliever to Knowles, and Fernandez was a mere journeyman. Short's real motivation in making the trade was not to improve the team, but to upgrade his own bottom line. As part of his deal with the A's, Short convinced Oakland owner Charlie Finley to give him $300,000. Unfortunately, Williams couldn't fill out his lineup with money; he needed lots of good players, and preferably younger ones.

Williams also felt that the Senators needed to expand their recruitment of Latino players, a belief that may have sprung in part from his own Mexican heritage. Williams wanted Short to hire two former players of Latino descent, Minnie Minoso and Camilo Pascual, as full-time scouts who would specialize in searching the Caribbean.[2] The manager pitched the idea to Short, but the owner claimed he didn't have the finances to support two additions to the payroll.

As the season progressed, Williams began to phase out some of the remaining veteran players in favor of younger players who might bring some enthusiasm and hope to a dismal baseball setting. The youthful group of Senators included infielder Toby Harrah and outfielders Larry Biittner and Jeff Burroughs, the latter a future American League MVP. Not surprisingly, some of the older players chafed at Williams' decision to cut their playing time. Their displeasure with Williams extended into other areas, such as the manager's personality and his way of handling players. Several of the unhappy veterans formed an informal group that became known as the "Underminers Club." They criticized Williams in discussions amongst themselves and with members of the media.

One veteran, second baseman Bernie Allen, became known as "The Imperial Wizard" of the Underminers Club because of his extreme dislike of Williams. Playing the leading role among the dissidents, Allen became so disgruntled with Williams' managing approach that he threatened to retire if the Senators did not trade him after the season.[3] The Senators accommodated Allen, sending him to the New York Yankees for two minor league pitchers. After the trade, Allen tore into Williams publicly, referring to him as the "most egotistical" man he had ever met while accusing the manager of running the team like a "concentration camp."[4]

The general grousing of the veteran players, the questionable attitude of Denny McLain, the grand failure of the blockbuster trade with Detroit, and growing rumors about the future of the franchise conspired to make Williams' life in Washington difficult. As Senators beat writer Merrell Whittlesey noted, Williams did not seem to enjoy managing the team as much in 1971 as he had during his first two years at the helm.[5] The lightheartedness and sense of humor that Williams frequently exhibited in his earlier days as Senators manager had dissipated significantly during the summer of 1971.

Given the disastrous developments of the season, it seemed only appropriate that 1971 would mark the final year of the Senators' franchise in Washington. On September 30, Williams and the Senators prepared to play their final game, with the New York Yankees providing the opposition. That game, scheduled for Washington's RFK Stadium, would turn out to be one of the most memorable, strange, and surreal evenings in major league history.

Only ten days earlier, Bob Short had received permission from his fellow American League owners to move the franchise to the deep South, specifically to Arlington, Texas. For several years, Short had complained about declining profits caused by a lack of civic support. He had also fretted about the conditions of his lease at RFK Stadium. On several occasions, he had threatened to move the Senators, with the Dallas–Ft. Worth area often the rumored destination.

Senators fans responded to the impending move by criticizing Short for failing to improve the team during his tenure as owner. Writers again pointed to the ill-fated Denny McLain deal as a primary reason for the ballclub's downfall in 1971 after a promising 86–76 campaign just two seasons earlier. Critics of Short would forever link the decline of the Senators with this disastrous deal.

In anticipation of potential fan unruliness, and perhaps outright violence, the city of Washington paid for fifty extra police officers to patrol RFK Stadium for the final game in franchise history. The city's fears soon became justified. A crowd of 14,460 fans paid their way into RFK Stadium, but an additional 4,000 fans barged through the turnstiles without tickets in order to bear witness to the Senators' final game. Fans carried large "anti-Short" banners, some of which contained profane language and were later removed by police officers. One particularly large banner, featuring the words, "Bob Short Stinks," hung vertically from the outfield rafters. Shortly after security demanded the banner be taken down, a group of fans hastily prepared another handwritten banner that made the following insistent declaration: "Bob Short Still Stinks." The second banner drew roars of approval from the fans at RFK. Another group of fans went a step further, constructing a stuffed dummy that bore a likeness to Short. The angry Senators' fans hung Short in effigy over a stadium railing.

In the days leading up to the final game, most of the Senators' younger players had expressed indifference over the forthcoming move to Arlington. One player and one manager, however, were particularly upset over the decision to shift the franchise. Frank "Hondo" Howard, the Senators' most popular player had told reporters in recent days that he did not want to leave Washington to play in Texas. Instead, Howard expressed a wish to be traded. "I'm sure Dallas deserves a team," Howard told the *Sporting News*, "but I'm sorry it had to be ours."[6] Of all of the Senators' players, the prospects of playing the final game at RFK Stadium clearly hit Hondo the hardest. While Williams did not feel such close ties to Washington as Howard did, he was not pleased, either. Although Williams publicly defended Short's decision to move the team and seemed to believe the owner's cries of poverty in Washington, he groused about the prospect of moving to a new city, where he would have to deal with a new set of media members and another round of introductory press conferences and gatherings.

Short, perhaps out of fear for his safety, did not attend the final game. Neither did team vice president Joe Burke, who was busy conducting business in Texas. Commissioner Bowie Kuhn and American League president Joe Cronin also decided against putting in appearances at RFK Stadium. One of the few notable baseball celebrities who did decide to attend the game was Hall of Famer Bucky Harris, a member of the Senators' all-time team. And of course there was Ted Williams, the lone legendary figure *in uniform* for the final game in Washington.

The early events of the game did not please Williams or Washington fans, with the latter staging periodic outbursts against Short, threatening to halt the game prematurely. Home runs by Rusty Torres, Bobby Murcer, and Roy White gave the opposition Yankees a 5–1 lead heading into the bottom of the sixth inning. As Frank Howard prepared to face Yankee left-hander Mike Kekich, fans cheered wildly for the likeable Washington slugger. Howard had earned the nickname, "The Capitol Punisher," for the way he "punished" fastballs that captured too much of his strike zone—a strike zone that had become smaller and more defined under the tutelage of Ted Williams. Kekich threw fastball after fastball during the confrontation with Howard, until the southpaw finally delivered a hittable pitch, which Hondo crushed on a line into the left-field stands. As Howard circled the bases to complete his 26th home run of the season, the onlookers at RFK responded with a standing ovation that lasted several thundering minutes. Fans repeatedly called for Howard to make a curtain call, which he finally delivered at the behest of several of his teammates and even Williams, who wanted his star player to enjoy the spotlight this bittersweet night. As Merrell Whittlesey described in the *Washington Evening Star*, Howard's heroics provided the evening's grandest moment. "Washington's lifetime in the majors almost ended with Hondo's homer," Whittlesey wrote. "The crowd gave him a standing ovation which lasted for several minutes and Howard had to be persuaded by manager Ted Williams and others to take two curtain calls, one to throw his helmet liner to the crowd, and the other to throw a kiss."[7] Howard then prepared to return to the dugout. In one of the rarest on-field displays in the game's history, the six-foot, nine-inch giant openly cried as he stepped back into the Senator dugout. The moments surrounding Howard's home run represented the high point of an evening otherwise filled with anger, disgust, and violence.

"Utopia," Howard exclaimed after the game, when asked to describe his feelings upon blasting the Kekich fastball into the left field stands. "It's the biggest thrill I've ever had, and anything else I'll ever do in baseball will be anticlimactic," Howard declared to the *Sporting News*. "I've hit a home run in the World Series, but nothing will ever top this. I'll take it to my grave."[8] Williams, who liked Howard and considered him the strongest hitter he had ever seen—even more so than Jimmie Foxx or Mickey Mantle—had to be pleased by Hondo's heroics on such an emotional night.

Howard's home run launched a four-run Senator rally, which tied the game at 5–5. In the bottom of the eighth inning, Dave Nelson and Tom Ragland reached on Yankee errors, and came around to score on a single by Howard's defensive replacement at first base, Tom McCraw, and a sacrifice fly by Elliott Maddox.

Thanks to the two-run rally, the Senators carried a 7–5 lead into the ninth inning. With two outs, Washington left-hander Joe Grzenda prepared to face Yankee second baseman Horace Clarke. With the Senators seemingly moments away from a victory in their final game, hordes of fans began vaulting over the retaining walls and proceeded to swarm the playing field. As Yankees and Senators players ran for cover, some of the fans ran directly toward the bases, pulling them out of the ground, spikes and all. Others tore home plate from its sockets. Another group of fans climbed the bullpen roof and removed lights and letters from the scoreboard. Hundreds of fans ripped out sods of grass from RFK Stadium's playing surface. Most of the intruders sought various kinds of special mementos that would remind them of the final game in the history of Senators baseball. It was the kind of scene that Ted Williams had never before witnessed during his long tenure in the game.

The storming of the field by hundreds of fans came as no surprise to the Senators' players. After the eighth inning, Washington's relief corps had cleared the bullpen and made its way for the runway leading to the clubhouse. With the playing surface reduced to shambles, and players fearing for their safety, the umpires huddled to discuss the situation. At 10:11 P.M., the umpires' crew chief, Jim Honochick, decided to call the game a forfeit and awarded the Yankees a 9–0 victory.[9] As part of baseball rules, all statistics from the game counted in the official day-by-day records, but neither a winning nor a losing pitcher was credited. (According to *The New Dickson Baseball Dictionary*, the score 9–0 was chosen because many early baseball games were forfeited when one of the teams could not field nine players.) It was the first game to be forfeited in the major leagues since 1954.[10]

Much to his credit, Yankees team president Michael Burke had decided to make the trip to Washington and attend the final game at RFK. In one of the more sportsmanlike gestures in baseball history, Burke asked the umpires to overturn the forfeit and award the Senators a win in their final game. Honochick asked Cronin to decide the matter, but the league president said the forfeit—and therefore the Yankees' 9–0 win—would stand. The Senators' last game, in all too typical fashion, had ended in defeat, which would be charged to Williams' mark as manager of the team. The latest loss left Williams with a record thirty-three games below .500 for the season, putting him and the sorry Senators in second-to-last place in the American League East. It was certainly not the way that Williams wanted to finish what had started out as such a promising tenure in Washington.

NOTES

1. Ron Bergman, "Trade Revives McLain's Enthusiasm," *Sporting News*, March 18, 1972, 32.

2. Whitfield, *Kiss It Goodbye*, 225.

3. Ibid., 55.

4. Ibid., 196.

5. Merrell Whittlesey, *The Sporting News Official Baseball Guide for 1972* (St. Louis: The Sporting News, 1972), 138.

6. Merrell Whittlesey, "Washington Sad, Shocked, and Bitter," *Sporting News*, October 9, 1971, 8.

7. Merrell Whittlesey, *Washington Evening Star*, October 1, 1971.

8. Jerome Holtzman, *The Sporting News Official Baseball Guide for 1972* (St. Louis: The Sporting News, 1972), 306.

9. Smith, *Storied Stadiums*, 305.

10. Holtzman, *The Sporting News Official Baseball Guide for 1972*, 306.

THE LONELY RANGER

The back of Ted Williams' 1972 Topps baseball card offered the manager—and his new-look Texas Rangers—some hope for the coming season.

> "The Splendid Splinter" has cause to be optimistic about the future. With such veterans on the club as Frank Howard, Denny McLain and Don Mincher plus youngsters the likes of Pete Broberg, Lenny Randle, Jeff Burroughs and Larry Biittner in addition to Ted Kubiak, Rich Hand, Roy Foster & Hal King acquired in off season trades, the future looks bright in Texas.

Unfortunately, the developments of the strike-delayed 1972 season did not fulfill such an optimistic prophesy by the copy writers at Topps. Denny McLain never put on a Texas Rangers uniform in the regular season, failing to last the duration of spring training with Williams and owner Bob Short, who decided to peddle the right-hander and his hefty contract. Short traded the onetime superstar to the A's, who needed a veteran starter while Vida Blue held out in a contract dispute, for young right-handers Jim Panther and Don Stanhouse. Outfielder Roy Foster, expected to provide some much-needed power, was also dealt during the spring, sent to the Indians for an outfielder named Ted Ford. Several other veterans failed to last the season. Distracted by his player representative duties during the spring training strike talks, Don Mincher found himself buried in an early season slump, which placed him on the trade block. Like McLain, Mincher and Ted Kubiak moved on to the A's, as part of a mid-season trade that marked the beginning of a housecleaning for the out-of-contention Rangers. Texas also traded the aging Frank Howard, who had been an institution in Washington but had held out during his first spring training with the Rangers because of a contract dispute. Hondo then proceeded to hit only nine home runs in 287 at-bats, with his plate struggles resulting in him being sold to the playoff-bound Tigers for the waiver price.

Even the Rangers' prized youngsters failed to make the grade for Williams and the Rangers. Lenny Randle, who started the season at second base, batted only .193 and descended into reduced status as a utility infielder. Singles-hitting first baseman–outfielder Larry Biittner batted a meager .259 without power. Jeff Burroughs, the heir apparent to Howard as the team's leading power hitter, suffered a back injury that limited him to a .185 average and only 65 at-bats; he also drew the ire of Williams for excessively "celebrating" his 21st birthday and for growing his hair too long.[1] With his offense flailing at all levels, Williams tried to compensate by using the sacrifice bunt and the stolen base as weapons. The Rangers managed to lead the league in stolen bases, but their team speed couldn't compensate for the team's .217 batting average—the worst in the league—and a glaring lack of power.

Despite a slight improvement in the team's ERA, the Rangers' young pitching also frustrated Williams. Right-hander Pete Broberg, considered an ace-in-the-making and once compared to Hall of Famer Bob Feller by Williams himself, stumbled to a record of 5–12 with a bloated ERA of 4.29, the highest of all the full-time starters. (Broberg would never live up to the Feller association; while some observers criticized Williams for Broberg's inability to develop, the former no. 1 draft choice out of Dartmouth also struggled in later stints with the Brewers, Cubs, and A's, where he continued to fail under a variety of pitching coaches and managers.) Of the younger pitchers, only right-hander Rich Hand showed any real promise under Williams, winning ten games and posting a respectable ERA of 3.32.

Williams' evaluation of certain players also came under question in 1972. He repeatedly promised that veteran catcher Hal King would hit, solving a perennial problem—lack of offense from behind the plate. Despite Williams' faith in King, the lefty-swinging receiver floundered both at the bat and in the field, and eventually earned a demotion to Triple-A Denver. The lack of development on the part of King frustrated Williams, as did a host of injuries that claimed outfielder Elliott Maddox and pitchers Dick Bosman, Casey Cox, and Jim Shellenback.

It wasn't just the continued labor of losing that wore on Williams. With the Senators moving to Arlington in 1972, Williams began to lose interest in managing period. The constant and often oppressive heat, along with the frequent rainstorms that plagued Arlington throughout the summer, seemed to take their toll on Williams, who had grown to like the diverse cultural life that the city of Washington offered. Perhaps because of his growing unhappiness, Williams became more distant at the ballpark, electing not to mingle with fans as he had in Washington.[2] And Texas fans didn't warm to Williams, with the Rangers drawing only 7,818 more fans than the Senators had during their final year in Washington.

Williams also continued to suffer in his communications with his players, a growing source of trouble that reached another boiling point during the summer of 1972. Just as in 1971, a number of players became disenchanted with Williams. The players complained that Williams was a perfectionist, a man who expected too much from ballplayers not blessed with the same kind of talent that "The Kid" possessed during his Hall of Fame tenure in Boston. They became increasingly annoyed with his sermons on fishing and tales of old-time ballplayers, questioning the relevance that such stories had to their current-day fortunes. They also became angry when Williams questioned their intelligence or insulted their playing abilities, sometimes going as far as to suggest a new line of work outside of baseball.[3] In particular, Williams showed little respect for pitchers, more than once referring to them as "stupid."[4]

Clearly, the atmosphere in Texas had become entirely hostile, with feelings of dislike between the players and Williams becoming mutual. Similarly unpleasant sentiments developed in the relationship between Ted and owner Bob Short, who insisted on rushing young players to the major leagues against the advice of his manager. Short also refused to adhere to his manager's advice on possible trades, a tendency that frustrated Williams. Williams' overall level of discontent reached its high point on September 30, the concluding day to a month that saw the Rangers post a dreadful record of 3–23. With the wretched Rangers on the verge of losing their fifteenth straight game, Williams announced his resignation, effective at the end of the regular season. Four days after the announcement, Williams watched the Rangers lose their 100th game on the final day of the season's calendar, and then officially stepped aside.

Although Williams still had one year remaining on his five-year contract, the torment of Texas' fifty-four-win season convinced Ted that it was time to give up the managerial reigns. Unlike the end of his playing career, Williams' swan song as manager took place without drama or fanfare. Frustrated and weary, he intended not to manage again, leaving behind a record of 273 wins and 364 losses and a winning percentage of .429.

Williams' managerial days appeared to have come to an end. But less than two years after his departure from the Rangers, rumors circulated that Williams might return to the managing ranks. Out in Oakland, controversial A's owner

Charlie Finley now needed a manager after the resignation of Dick Williams, an accomplished skipper who had grown tired of the owner's constant interference and continuing efforts at embarrassing players. In conducting a search for Dick Williams' replacement, Finley wanted a manager with star appeal, a big name who would bring Finley and the A's a large degree of publicity. According to at least one report, Finley appeared to be considering several intriguing candidates, including former Rangers skipper Whitey Herzog (Ted's successor), current California Angels outfielder Frank Robinson, and three retired stars: Satchel Paige, Maury Wills—and Ted Williams himself.[5] Finley would have loved to hire a legendary figure like Williams, whose hiring would have generated scores of headlines and whose presence and name value would have attracted fans to the Oakland Coliseum. Yet, Williams was not interested in returning to managing, and probably had little desire in working for an owner as intrusive and demanding as Finley. As a result, Williams did not even interview for the vacant managerial position in Oakland. He remained on the sidelines, never to manage again.

NOTES

1. Whitfield, *Kiss It Goodbye*, 212–214.
2. Merle Heryford, *The Sporting News Official Baseball Guide for 1973* (St. Louis: The Sporting News, 1973), 37.
3. Mike Shropshire, *Seasons in Hell: With Billy Martin, Whitey Herzog and "The Worst Baseball Team in History"—The 1973–1975 Texas Rangers* (New York: Donald I. Fine Books, 1996), 78–79.
4. Whitfield, *Kiss It Goodbye*, 51.
5. *Sporting News*, date unknown.

RETIREMENT, RESPECT, AND
REQUIEM FOR A LEGEND

Williams' career as a manager had begun promisingly in 1969 before deteriorating into an environment of losing and discontent over the next three seasons. His tenure as manager of the Senators and Rangers prompted a mixed bag of reviews. Some observers preferred to focus on the short-term success that he had enjoyed in improving so many mediocre players in his first year, earning him deserved acclaim as Manager of the Year. Others pointed to the lack of long-term development of the younger Senators-Rangers players, and an eroding clubhouse atmosphere that had grown cold and hostile. On the surprising side, the often temperamental Williams had shown surprising patience with American League umpires, restraining his anger in most on-field disputes and never once earning an ejection in four years on the job.[1]

The days of managing had come to an end, but Williams couldn't stay away from the ballpark—or the Boston Red Sox. After his resignation as Rangers manager, Williams regularly made appearances at the Red Sox spring training site and at Fenway Park during the regular season. In 1978, Tom Yawkey officially made him a permanent part of the Red Sox organization, giving him the lifetime title of "instructor."[2] In making his annual trip to the Red Sox spring training site in Winter Haven, Florida, Williams sported a Boston uniform and offered hitting advice to both minor leaguers and major leaguers in the Red Sox system.

During his retirement years, Williams became a kind of unofficial guru of hitting, a trusted aide to Red Sox hitters who desperately sought pieces of advice that the greatest hitter in the game's history might be able to pass off to them. In addition to emerging as a sage for professional players, Williams became a frequent magnet of counsel to the amateur baseball world, both to young players at the scholastic levels or to the fathers of such budding young stars. As part of the initial stage of instruction, one that might be considered unconventional, Williams strongly recommended that a young player make an effort to learn about the sport through the written word. "Well, of course," Williams told the Hall of Fame, "he's got to try to read as much as he can about the game. That's the downfall [for] most players in baseball."[3] Williams felt that by learning more about the game's history and the philosophies of playing baseball, players could only improve their mental grasp of the sport's intricacies.

In speaking to others about the art of refining one's baseball skills, Williams found a common theme of complaint: *My fielding is fine, but I need work with my hitting.* "There you go, that's the answer [from] pretty near everybody," Williams revealed to the Hall of Fame. Even celebrities sounded a similar refrain.

> "I can field pretty good," that's what President [George H. W.] Bush told me. He loved to talk about hitting and baseball. Apparently he was the captain of the Yale team. He said, "I was a pretty good fielder, but I had a little trouble hitting." Now that's the story of [the last] 80 years. His dad takes his kid out, the kid fields pretty good, and all of a sudden he starts to [move up to] a better league. Now he's not hitting like he used to until finally he doesn't even make the baseball team. Finally his father said, "Let's start playing golf." So that could be the next step or he might be an ungainly tall guy, so he might say, "Let's try basketball." That's the downfall of most young baseball players. Now [hitting is] a hard thing to do and you can talk for a month and a half to some guys and you wouldn't teach them one thing about hitting. It's a hard thing to coach, you have to have some experience to do it, and you got to have some ability, got to have good eyes, and you have to have athletic ability where you can swing coordinated and quick. Making good contact with a round ball and a round bat, even if you know what's coming, is hard to do. That seems to be the one major thing that all young players have difficulty with. Why? It's the hardest thing to do in baseball. Maybe it's the one hardest thing to do in sports.[4]

As Williams explained to the Hall of Fame, other parts of the game come far more naturally for most players. "[For example,] a guy can run like a deer," said Williams. "You don't even have to scout it; you can just see it and that's it; he'll never lose that until he's 40 years old. . . . Speed has no slumps, if you've ever heard that expression, boy is that true. Speed doesn't have any slumps."[5] In contrast, even the greatest of hitters must periodically flail away during times of ineptitude in the batter's box.

Williams also believed that good young hitters needed to test themselves against the best possible competition. "For example, if a young kid is tearing down the fences, I believe in pushing him," Williams told the Hall of Fame. "Put him in a tougher league—don't let him burn this league up—he's proven he can do that. Then he gets a little bit higher and he has a little stalling period there, but if you keep pushing him all the time where nothing is really easy, he's got to bear down to succeed, to get better, and compete. I think he progresses better in the long run this way. No question."[6]

Unlike many old-time players who continually pine for the days of their youthful prime, when they claimed that the "game was far better in their day," Williams expressed admiration for modern-day players right up until the time of this death. "You know what," Williams told the Hall of Fame in 2000, "I think baseball is potentially as good now as it [ever was]; it's got the athletes to be as good as it's ever been. You've got big, strong, powerful kids that can run that are athletes and make plays in the outfield that I never saw until the last 20 years. Strong, hit them a mile. [Maybe] they haven't played as much as some kids maybe, 40 to 50 years ago. But they are outstanding in hitting home runs."[7]

While Williams freely heaped praise on modern-day players, the baseball community—both young and old—continued to show a growing appreciation for him throughout the 1990s. During the summer of 1991, the Red Sox honored their long-retired star with "Ted Williams Day" at Fenway Park. As Williams acknowledged the cheers of the crowd, he parted ways with a vow that he had made many years earlier. Displaying a gentler side that he had often hidden in the past, a forgiving Williams finally tipped his cap to the Fenway fans for the first time since 1952.

In some ways, the tipping of the cap, although a relatively effortless gesture, marked a watershed moment of significant change in Williams' public persona. As a player, Williams was cantankerous and irritable, occasionally with the fans and often with the media. He was often perceived as moody and unnecessarily difficult—and rightly so. Yet, in his post-playing days, he began to develop an outward maturity, a willingness to show his lighter, more charming side. The conversion had actually begun as early as 1969, when Williams first became a major league manager. In his first press conference after being named skipper of the Washington Senators, he had displayed a vibrant enthusiasm, a keen sense of humor, and a sincere willingness to relate personally to members of the media, rather than maintaining that cold separation that usually existed between writer and superstar. And now, by the early 1990s, Ted Williams had completed that remarkable transformation, by showing a willingness to forget bitter feelings of the past and make peace with those fans who loved him, flaws and all.

Williams' willingness to show the healthier side of his character—his humor, his zeal for life, and his sincere interest in others—may have contributed to the increased recognition he received during the 1990s. In 1991, President George H. W. Bush invited Williams to a White House ceremony and awarded him the celebrated Medal of Freedom, considered the nation's highest civilian honor. In 1997, a lesser but still prestigious award also came his way. The Society for American Baseball Research (SABR), an organization devoted to the advancement of statistical, historical, and current-day baseball knowledge but sometimes criticized for its members' cold, impassioned view of the game and picayune obsession with statistics and facts, rewarded Williams with one of its highest honors. SABR officially presented Williams with its "Hero of Baseball Award." For years, Sabermetricians had recognized and praised Williams as statistically the best hitter in the history of the game, but this award represented more than a recognition of cold, hard numbers. It was an appreciation of a man who was not only a great baseball player, but also a tireless worker who pursued excellence, a vital ambassador for the National Pastime, and a selfless, courageous hero of war.

Unfortunately, the 1990s also brought Ted a series of heath problems. In February 1994, he suffered a stroke, the first of several over the next few years. The first stroke affected his motor skills, which eventually returned, but also left his vision badly damaged. As a result, Williams could not perform simple actions as quickly as he had in the past, such as signing autographs. "I can sign," Williams told *Boston Globe* sportswriter Dan Shaughnessy. "But I need more time now. I used to whip 'em out pretty good. I need more time and I've got to make sure I get it [the autograph] in the right place."[8]

In spite of growing health concerns, Williams remained active in his support of the Red Sox official charity, the Jimmy Fund. In 1995, he traveled to Boston to attend both the dedication of the new "Ted Williams Tunnel," located under the Boston Harbor, and a fundraising event for the Dana-Farber Cancer Institute. At the evening fundraiser, he initiated the ".406 Club," a foundation that would eventually raise an additional $2 million for the Jimmy Fund.[9]

In July 1999, Williams made what turned out to be his final trip to the Dana-Farber Institute, where he visited with a number of ailing children. As with all of his other visits, he did so quietly, seeking no publicity or media coverage. Later that month, another appearance by Williams would not allow him to elude the spotlight. Prior to the 1999 All Star Game at Fenway Park, an 81-year-old Williams rode around the ballpark's warning track in a golf cart before making an unforgettable stop near the mound, where he threw out the ceremonial first pitch. He was joined by thirty-one all-time greats, along with many of the game's current-day stars, including Tony Gwynn and Cal Ripken Jr. At one point, the public address announcer asked the All-Stars to return to their dugouts, but the players refused, not wanting to cut short their visit with "The Kid." While many contemporary baseball players have been rightfully accused of being ignorant of the game's history, these stars wanted to experience Ted Williams first-hand— by touching him, by talking to him, by being close to him.

In turn, Williams wanted to connect with the current-day stars who had taken the time to gather around him on this indelible summer night. The group of stars included St. Louis Cardinals slugger Mark McGwire, who had just become the game's single-season home-run king by hitting 70 home runs the previous season. Williams reportedly asked McGwire, "Do you ever smell the wood burn?"[10] It was an interesting question, but there was no word as to McGwire's response.

The gathering collection of contemporary All-Stars at Fenway that night also included the Red Sox own current-day star, Nomar Garciaparra. Williams and Garciaparra had become friends, in part because Ted so admired Garciaparra's abilities. It was yet another example of Williams' humility; he rarely expressed resentment of the modern-day player; instead generously offering praise and support, both through the media and in face-to-face conversations. In turn, Garciaparra sought out Williams for advice, regarding him as a confidante of the highest caliber.

Given Williams' age and his deteriorating physical state, many baseball observers regarded his appearance at the All Star Game as a king of public swan song. Sadly, his condition only worsened over the next three years, resulting in several extended stays at Florida hospitals. Plagued by congestive heart failure, his lengthy illness persisted, at times resulting in debilitating strokes. One of the strokes left him almost completely blind in one of his eyes. In the year 2000, doctors installed a pacemaker to regulate Williams' heartbeat. Unfortunately, the pacemaker did not work as well as his physicians would have liked, necessitating a long operation on his heart the following year. In January of 2001, Williams underwent grueling open-heart surgery that lasted nine hours; the procedure left him so weakened that he remained hospitalized until the end of August, when Ted returned home.

Shortly after his return home, three of his closest friends in baseball paid him a memorable visit, one that became a subject of a popular book written by noted sports author David Halberstam. The visitors were former Red Sox teammates, Bobby Doerr, Dom DiMaggio, and Johnny Pesky, who were all taken aback by how thin and gaunt their friend looked. Yet, they talked to Ted and reminisced, all the while expressing hope that he would get better.

Unfortunately, his condition did not improve. On July 5, 2002, Williams went into cardiac arrest and was brought to Citrus County Memorial Hospital, located near his home in Crystal River, Florida. At 8:49 A.M. Ted Williams passed away, finally succumbing to the multitude of ailments that had overwhelmed him in his later years. He was 83.

Reaction came swiftly from the baseball world, both from those he had played with and against during his iconic career. "Ted was a great team player," said Doerr, his former teammate and longtime friend. "He wanted to win. He patted everyone on the back. He took the pressure off the rest of the players. We were very close friends. We knew each other as 18-year-olds in San Diego. We would go to movies quite a bit, we'd talk fishing and we'd talk baseball. He was a loyal friend. He was ahead of his time in baseball in many ways."[11]

"He was one of my best friends on earth and the greatest hitter I ever faced," said Bob Feller, who had played his career as an opponent of Williams but nonetheless became close to the Red Sox great. "I faced a lot of guys, including Lou Gehrig. He was a great friend to my wife Anne and me. He was a great American."[12] Like Williams, Feller had served proudly in the U.S. military during World War II.

Even players from the National League felt Williams' impact, both personally and professionally. "Ted Williams was a great friend. I mostly remember how he helped me when I first came to Phoenix," said Willie Mays. "He spent time talking to me about hitting, even though he played on another team. I'm very, very sorry to hear of his passing. . . . This is a great loss."[13] A teammate of Mays, one who shared a milestone with Williams, also received important advice from The Kid. "Ted helped me a lot when I first started," said Willie McCovey.

> He gave me a lot of tips on hitting. I met him in Scottsdale during my first spring training with the Giants. He was still with the Red Sox. I used to pick his brain, being a rookie and all, and he was willing to give me advice. I always credit him with helping me. All of his advice turned out to be good for me—bat selection, weights of bats, everything. He and I were the same height. He was a student of pitchers. I applied much of what he told me about his theories on hitting and it worked for me. We ended up with the same number of home runs and that means a lot to me.[14]

While the careers of Mays and McCovey overlapped with Williams, younger players of later generations also felt his influence. "I met him my first spring training," says Carlton Fisk, who began his major league career with the Red Sox in 1969. "He was very much involved early in the spring. He came right over to me. He was loud, aggressive and assured. He comes over and was asking me questions about hitting. Here I am, an 18-year old! It's a sad day for all of baseball. Knowing Ted, everyone was hanging on to yesteryear through him. It's a sad day."[15]

Later that evening, just a few hours after the news of Williams' passing, the Red Sox prepared to play a home game against the Tigers. The flag flew at half-staff, while the scoreboard at Fenway Park featured a short message: "AT BAT, NUMBER 9, BATTING .406."

A few weeks later, on the evening of July 22, the Red Sox held an extended public ceremony at Fenway Park, with all proceeds from the ticketed event earmarked to benefit the Jimmy Fund. The two-hour program, billed as "Ted Williams: A Celebration of An American Hero," featured appearances by retired astronaut and Korean War veteran John Glenn, and a slew of former Red Sox standouts, including Dom DiMaggio, Johnny Pesky, Rico Petrocelli, Jim Rice, Luis Tiant, and Carl Yastrzemski. In addition to staging "nine innings" of spoken tributes, the Red Sox carefully placed a number of visual symbols throughout the ballpark, including markers that bore numbers such as "9," in honor of his uniform number, and ".406," commemorating his historic batting mark of 1941. In one of the most memorable scenes from the ceremony, Ted's friend, Nomar Garciaparra, kneeled down on the Fenway Park turf and tilted his head downward in a sign of respect for his departed advisor.[16]

Williams' death not only sparked a remarkably intense, nationwide period of mourning, but unfortunately also resulted in a controversial family in-fight regarding the disposal of his body. One of his two daughters, Bobby Jo Williams Ferrell (born to his first wife, Doris Soule), pointed to his written Last Will and Testament, and said that her father had expressed a wish to have his body cremated. Williams' son, John Henry Williams, and his other daughter, Claudia Williams (both born to his third wife, Dolores Wettach) claimed that their father had changed his mind and instead wanted to have his body "frozen" in a cryonics lab as a way of preserving his DNA for future use, or possibly to be "revived" at a later date. In December 2002, the matter was settled, at least temporarily, when Bobby Jo dropped her objections due to financial problems and allowed John Henry to proceed with his plans. Part of Williams' body remains in a cryonics lab in Scottsdale, Arizona, where some observers, including Williams' friend, Buzz Hamon, have criticized both the lab's procedures and its sanitary conditions.

The distastefulness and ugliness surrounding the entire episode did not befit the legacy of Ted Williams. He does not deserve to be remembered for such a controversy. Instead, he should be—and probably will be—remembered for accomplishing a goal that few baseball players have ever attained: achieving an iconic status that transcends the sport, allowing him to have an impact on widely varied groups of the American public. Baseball fans will remember him as arguably the game's greatest hitter, fishermen will recall his exploits with a rod and reel, and veterans of war will remember his dedicated service to the military during two major wars. Even those segments of the American population that fail to fit any of these categories will make some connection to Williams, based on his rugged good looks, his similarities to John Wayne's confidence, and the general charm of his later years. It's rare for an American sports figure to reach so many diverse groups within our culture, but Williams succeeded in doing just that.

Just how famous and far-reaching was Ted Williams? In 1980, longtime Detroit sportswriter Joe Falls conducted a random poll of 100 people walking the streets in Deerfield Beach, Florida. Falls asked each one of the participants a simple question. "Do you know who Ted Williams is?" Each one of the 100 respondents said, "Yes."[17] Yes, they had all heard of Ted Williams. Unlike most players, whose names fade into oblivion after retirement, Williams' accomplishments as a war hero, legendary hitter, and charismatic celebrity had made him an authentic American icon.

NOTES

1. Whitfield, *Kiss It Goodbye*, 54.
2. Shaughnessy, "Ted Williams: A Life Remembered—Plenty on His Plate," online edition.
3. Interview with Ted Williams, conducted by Jeff Idelson of the National Baseball Hall of Fame, 2000.
4. Ibid.
5. Ibid.
6. Ibid.
7. Ibid.
8. Shaughnessy, "The Kid," 76.
9. Shaughnessy, "Ted Williams: A Life Remembered—Plenty on His Plate," online edition.
10. Smith, *Storied Stadiums*, 494.
11. National Baseball Hall of Fame Press Release, July 5, 2002.

12. Ibid.
13. Ibid.
14. Ibid.
15. Ibid.
16. Wendel, *The New Face of Baseball*, 175.
17. Shaughnessy, "The Kid," 76.

EPILOGUE:
MAKING OF A LEGEND

In Ted Williams' first major league season, his outspoken tendencies made him a quotable favorite among some local and national sportswriters, while making heads shake among the more conservative members of the northeastern sports-writing brethren. Increasingly, beginning with his second season when his power numbers fell off and brought criticism from fans and media, Williams' brash-ness and arrogance made him an easy target for some of the most outspoken writers in the Boston area. In 1940, an interview with Austen "Duke" Lake of the *Boston American* put Williams squarely on the firing line. Upset with insin-uations from Red Sox manager Joe Cronin that his current back injury might not be serious enough to prevent him from playing, Williams ranted and raved to Lake about his general unhappiness with Boston management, his teammates, the media, and even the fans. The subsequent article resulted in a firestorm of angry reaction, including a scathing column from Dave Egan of the *Boston Record*. Often outrageous in tone, Egan initiated what some would label a ca-reer obsession—criticizing Williams at every turn in an effort to turn fans against the local baseball hero. Egan continued his negative portrayals of Williams for the rest of his writing career.

The criticisms put forth by Egan, Austen Lake, and other members of the Boston sporting press made Williams distrustful of writers. Establishing a wall of separation between himself and local sportswriters, Williams became more reticent in his dealings with the press. When he did talk to the media, he rarely smiled and often made snide remarks that made his dislike of sportswriters read-ily apparent.

Williams' unwillingness to act cordially contributed to the press' general perception of him as moody, irritable, and downright difficult. Such perceptions quickly transferred to the general public, which at that time relied heavily on newspaper and magazine coverage in following the fortunes of baseball and its star players. Williams' unwillingness to tip his cap or acknowledge the fans in any other tangible way only cemented his reputation as aloof and unfriendly.

Unfortunately, some members of the media allowed personal feelings toward Williams to affect their evaluations of him as a player and their decisions to vote on postseason awards and honors. Some writers, like Dave Egan, criticized Williams for his unwillingness to be a "team player" by swinging at errant pitches with runners on base, for his reluctance to lay down bunts at appropriate times, and for his supposed lack of desire to improve his fielding skills. While Williams did win two American League Most Valuable Player Awards during his career, many objective analysts believe that he should have won the MVP award at least four times.

Nevertheless, the antagonistic relationship between Williams and the press did not cost him when it came time for Hall of Fame consideration. Williams earned election to the Cooperstown shrine on his first try, gaining an impressive 93.38 percent of the vote, well beyond the 75 percent minimum required for enshrinement. During his induction speech, Williams offered a plea on behalf of Negro Leagues players, expressing his wish that they be honored with plaques in Cooperstown. Williams' generous act of selflessness, coupled with his earlier heroism flying dangerous missions during the Korean War, began to change perceptions, at least in the minds of some, that he was merely an arrogant braggart who reveled in making enemies with the press. Clearly, a different side to Williams' character had emerged.

Williams' public persona continued to evolve during his tenure as a manager with the Washington Senators and Texas Rangers. Forced by the requirements of a managerial position to deal more readily with the media, Williams became more open to discussing his theories about baseball and, of course, the science of hitting. He allowed the media to gain insight into his thoughts and philosophies on sports, politics, and any number of current-day events. He still engaged in spats with writers from time to time, but those occurred less frequently and with less ferocity.

After resigning as manager, Williams seemed to mellow further. Freed from the pressures of a pennant race and from answering the second-guessing questions of sportswriters, Williams became even less cantankerous and more relaxed. He joked more often in magazine and television interviews, allowing readers and viewers to witness his keen sense of humor and general playfulness, characteristics that had usually been hidden from public view.

A watershed moment in the development of Williams' image occurred at the Hall of Fame in 1985. That year, the Hall invited Ted to Cooperstown for the unveiling of a life-size wooden sculpture depicting Williams in the midst of his classic left-handed swing. Overwhelmed by the beauty and precision of the piece, Williams began to cry openly. Photos of his emotional reaction appeared in a number of newspapers, revealing a very human side of his personality that he had often withheld from public view. From that moment on, Williams forged a much closer relationship with the institution in Cooperstown and began to attend every subsequent Hall of Fame ceremony until he was physically unable to do so. According to the Hall of Fame's chief curator, Ted Spencer, Williams was so touched by the sculpture and the Hall's decision to spotlight it prominently within the Museum that he assumed a warmer and friendlier aura during his Hall of Fame visits. Williams willingly participated in autograph signings, even signing for an impromptu gathering of Cooperstown fans at six o'clock in the morning. Such occurrences showed Williams at his finest—and provided a sign of things to come.

Throughout the late 1980s and the 1990s, Williams continued to grow in esteem, both with old-time sportswriters who remembered his previously ornery personality and younger fans who had never actually seen him play. Williams' charm, sense of humor, and sincere interest in the questions of others made him an appealing interview subject, whether it be as a guest on national TV or on a one-to-one fan-to-superstar basis. The level of regard only seemed to increase as an aging Williams became frail, weakened by a series of strokes and congestive heart failure. Williams seemed to reach his peak in popularity at the 1999 All Star Game, when many of baseball's current-day stars refused to leave the field so that they could spend additional time with the game's great hero and most popular living icon.

Even in death, Williams remains a popular topic of conversation within the American sports culture. Sadly, much of that interest stems from the morbid controversy over the disposal of his remains, which has spawned all too much distasteful humor while tainting the family's name. Yet, amongst the true fans of the game and those who believe that athletes can achieve iconic status, the name Ted Williams elicits far more favorable memories, ranging from vivid impressions of his artistic swing to images of his outgoing, life-loving personality.

A number of excellent sources have helped in writing this biography of Ted Williams. One of the most useful was William's own work, written with David Pietrusza, *Teddy Ballgame: My Life in Pictures*. Written toward the end of Williams' life, the book provides Ted's own perspectives and opinions about a number of important episodes in his professional career. Pietrusza, a fine and detailed writer, does solid work in editing and fine-tuning Williams' comments, which exhibit both his pride and his self-effacing nature, and further reinforced the popular image of Williams that evolved in the last decades of his life.

Another good source is *Ted Williams: The Pursuit of Perfection*, compiled by Bill Nowlin and Jim Prime, who interviewed almost every friend and close associate of Williams. Formatted as a series of oral histories, this volume provides a wide range of perspectives on Williams' intriguing personality and his dedication to standout performance. The book succeeds as a celebration of Williams' achievements, reaffirming much of the favorable notice he received during the later years of his life.

Ted Williams: A Portrait in Words and Pictures by Dick Johnson and Glenn Stout provides numerous statistical tables, including Williams' year-by-year batting numbers, his performances in each major league ballpark, and breakdowns against left-handed and right-handed pitching. Through its use of in-depth statistics, the book confirms Williams' status as arguably the greatest hitter of all time.

A number of full-length biographies have been written about the legendary Williams. One of the best is Michael Seidel's *Ted Williams: A Baseball Life*, a detailed volume that objectively explores both his childhood and his career in baseball. Ed Linn's *Hitter: The Life and Turmoils of Ted Williams*, although somewhat dated, also provides a thorough examination of Williams' career along with opinionated analysis of his personality. Both books show the complexity of Williams' character.

Surprisingly few books about Williams offer much insight into his managerial career with the Washington Senators. The exception is the colorful account *Kiss It Goodbye*, written by former Senators broadcaster Shelby Whitfield. As a close associate of Williams, Whitfield writes at length about his conversations with Ted while offering insight into his managerial approach and his relationships with a number of Senators players. It is both an entertaining and informative read, confirming both Williams' high baseball and cultural intelligence, along with his tendency to land in controversial situations.

Among periodicals, the most valuable have been *Sport* magazine, *Sports Illustrated*, and the *Sporting News*. Now defunct, *Sport* magazine carried a number of in-depth feature articles about Williams during his major league career. The articles are rich in quotations from Williams, helping to bring his personality and character to life.

Finally, a nonpublished source from the National Baseball Hall of Fame and Museum provided numerous direct quotations from Williams himself. In the year 2000, the Hall's vice-president of communications and education, Jeff Idelson, held a lengthy sit-down interview with Williams. As one of the last full-length interviews conducted with Williams, Idelson's insightful discussion covers almost every major highlight of Ted's career while also providing a vivid sampling of his animated and enthusiastic personality.

CAREER STATISTICS

Year	Club	League	G	AB	R	H	2B	3B
1936	San Diego	Pacific Coast	42	107	18	29	8	2
1937	San Diego	Pacific Coast	138	454	66	132	24	2
1938	Minneapolis	Amer. Assoc.	148	528	130*	193	30	9
1939	Boston	American	149	565	131	185	44	11
1940&	Boston	American	144	561	134*	193	43	14
1941	Boston	Eastern	143	456	135*	185	33	3
1942	Boston	American	150	522	141*	186	34	5
1943	In Military Service							
1944	In Military Service							
1945	In Military Service							
1946	Boston	American	150	514	142*	176	37	8
1947	Boston	American	156	528	125*	181	40	9
1948	Boston	American	137	509	124	188	44*	3
1949	Boston	American	155**	566	150*	194	39*	3
1950	Boston	American	89	334	82	106	24	1
1951	Boston	American	148	531	109	169	28	4
1952+	Boston	American	6	10	2	4	0	1
1953+	Boston	American	37	91	17	37	6	0
1954	Boston	American	117	386	93	133	23	1
1955	Boston	American	98	320	77	114	21	3
1956	Boston	American	136	400	71	138	28	2
1957	Boston	American	132	420	96	163	28	1
1958	Boston	American	129	411	81	135	23	2

Year	Club	League	G	AB	R	H	2B	3B	HR	RBI	BA	PO	A	E	FA
1959	Boston	American	103	272	32	69	15	0	10	43	.254	94	4	3	.970
1960	Boston	American	113	310	56	98	15	0	29	72	.316	131	6	1	.993
Major League Totals—19 years			2292	7706	1798	2654	525	71	521	1839	.344	4158	140	113	.974
Minor League Totals—3 years			328	1089	214	354	62	13	66	251		546	32	20	

+ spent most of the year in military service

& appeared in one game as a pitcher

* indicates league leader

** indicates tied for league lead

A = assists; AB = at-bats; BA = batting average; E = errors; FA = fielding average; G = games; H = hits; HR = home runs; PO = put-outs; R = runs; RBI = runs batted in; 2B = doubles; 3B = triples

WORLD SERIES STATISTICS

Year	Club	G	AB	R	H	2B	3B	HR	RBI	BA	PO	A	E	FA
1946	Boston	7	25	2	5	0	0	0	1	.200	16	2	0	1.000
Totals, 1 year—		7	25	2	5	0	0	0	1	.200	16	2	0	1.000

Source: *Baseball Register*, 1961; http://www.baseball-reference.com.

SELECTED BIBLIOGRAPHY

BIOGRAPHIES AND AUTOBIOGRAPHIES OF TED WILLIAMS

Johnson, Dick, and Glenn Stout. *Ted Williams: A Portrait in Words and Pictures*. New York: Walker and Company, 1991.

Linn, Ed. *Hitter: The Life and Turmoils of Ted Williams*. New York: Harcourt Brace, 1993.

Nowlin, Bill, and Jim Prime. *Ted Williams: The Pursuit of Perfection*. Champaign, IL: Sports Publishing, 2002.

Seidel, Michael. *Ted Williams: A Baseball Life*. Chicago: Contemporary Books, 1991.

Whitfield, Shelby. *Kiss It Goodbye*. New York: Abelard-Schuman, 1973.

Williams, Ted, with David Pietrusza. *Teddy Ballgame: My Life in Pictures*. Toronto: Sport Classic Books, 2002.

BOOKS

Baseball Register: 1960 Edition. St. Louis: The Sporting News, 1960.

Baseball Register: 1961 Edition. St. Louis: The Sporting News, 1961.

Berry, Henry. *Baseball's Greatest Teams: The Boston Red Sox*. New York: Collier, 1975.

Bouton, Jim. *Ball Four: The Final Pitch*. Champaign, IL: Sports Publishing, 2000.

Bryant, Howard. *Shut Out: A Story of Race and Baseball in Boston*. New York and London: Routledge, 2002.

Chadwick, Bruce, and David T. Spindel. *The Boston Red Sox: Memories and Mementoes of New England's Team*. New York: Abbeville Press, 1992.

Davis, Allen F., "Williams, Theodore Samuel (Ted)." In *The Scribner Encyclopedia of American Lives: Sports Figures*. Edited by Arnold Markoe. New York: Charles Scribner's Sons, 2002.

Dickson, Paul. *The New Dickson Baseball Dictionary*. New York: Harcourt Brace, 1999.

Enders, Eric. *100 Years of the World Series*. New York: Barnes and Noble Books, 2003.

Heryford, Merle. *The Sporting News Official Baseball Guide for 1973*. St. Louis: The Sporting News, 1973.

Hollander, Zander. *The Complete Handbook of Baseball: 1971 Edition*. New York: Lancer Books, 1971.

Holtzman, Jerome. *The Sporting News Official Baseball Guide for 1972*. St. Louis: The Sporting News, 1972.

1998 Boston Red Sox Media Guide.

Pietrusza, David, et al., eds. *Baseball: The Biographical Encyclopedia*. Kingston, NY: Total Sports, 2000.

Riley, Dan, ed. *The Red Sox Reader*. New York: Houghton Mifflin, 1991.

Shaughnessy, Dan. *The Curse of the Bambino*. New York: EP Dutton Books, 1990.

Shropshire, Mike. *Seasons in Hell: With Billy Martin, Whitey Herzog and "The Worst Baseball Team in History"—The 1973–1975 Texas Rangers*. New York: Donald I. Fine Books, 1996.

Smith, Curt. *Storied Stadiums: Baseball's History Through Its Ballparks*. New York: Carroll and Graf, 2001.

Wendel, Tim. *The New Face of Baseball: The 100-Year Rise and Triumph of Latinos in America's Favorite Sport*. New York: Rayo Publishing, 2003.

Whittlesey, Merrell. *The Sporting News Official Baseball Guide for 1970*. St. Louis: The Sporting News, 1970.

ARTICLES

Bergman, Ron. "Trade Revives McLain's Enthusiasm." *Sporting News*, March 18, 1972, 32.

Caple, Jim. "Teddy Ballgame Left His Imprint on Many People." ESPN Web site, July 1, 2002.

Dreyspool, Joan Flynn. "Ted Williams." *Sports Illustrated*, August 1, 1955, 29.

Edes, Gordon. "Ted Williams: A Life Remembered—The Keyboards Were Always Spelling Trouble." *Boston Globe*, July 6, 2002, online edition.

Finnegan, Huck. *Boston American*, September 28, 1960.

Goldstein, Richard, and Robert McG. Thomas. "Ted Williams, Red Sox Slugger and Last To Hit .400, Dies at 83." *New York Times*, July 6, 2002, A1, D4.

Greene, Lee. "Ted Williams' Ten Greatest Days." *Sport*, June 1959, 26.

Hano, Arnold. "Mike Epstein: Somewhere Between Journeyman and Superstar." *Sport*, November 1972, 87.

Linn, Ed. "Growing Up With Ted." *Sport*, February 1966, 56.

————. "The Kid's Last Game." *Sport*, February 1961, 52–63.

McGinniss, Joe. "What Ted Williams Is Like Today." *Sport*, June 1969, 16.

Nowlin, Bill. "El Splinter Esplendido." *Boston Globe Magazine*, June 2, 2002, 15.

Ryan, Bob. "Ted Williams: A Life Remembered—His Desire Made Wish Come True." *Boston Globe*, July 6, 2002, online edition.

Shaughnessy, Dan. "The Kid." *Boston Globe*, August 5, 1994, 76.

————. "Ted Williams: A Life Remembered—Plenty on His Plate." *Boston Globe*, July 6, 2002, online edition.

"Ted Wins Recognition Hard Way." *Sporting News*, July 26, 1950, 12.

Underwood, John. "The Newest Senator in Town." *Sports Illustrated*, February 24, 1969, 20.

Updike, John. "Hub Fans Bid Kid Adieu." *The New Yorker*, October 22, 1960, 109.

Whittlesey, Merrell. "Ted, Nixon, Run Neck-and-Neck in Publicity Glare." *Sporting News*, May 31, 1969, 7.

————. "Ted's Tips Load Brinkman's Bat with Explosive Charge." *Sporting News*, May 24, 1969, 10.

————. *Washington Evening Star*, October 1, 1971.

————. "Washington Sad, Shocked, and Bitter." *Sporting News*, October 9, 1971, 8.

"Williams of the Red Sox Is Best Hitter." *Life*, September 1, 1941, 43.

WEB SITES

www.baseball-almanac.com

www.baseballhalloffame.org

www.baseballlibrary.com

www.baseball-reference.com

www.bostonherald.com

www.espn.com

www.retrosheet.org

www.sabr.org

http://stewthornley.net

www.tedwilliams.com

SPECIAL COLLECTIONS

Interview with Ted Williams, conducted by Jeff Idelson of the National Baseball Hall of Fame, February, 2000.

The National Baseball Hall of Fame Library (Ted Williams' player file).

The National Baseball Hall of Fame and Museum (press releases).

INDEX

About the Author

BRUCE MARKUSEN worked in education, programming, and research at the National Baseball Hall of Fame and Museum in Cooperstown, New York from 1994 to 2004. He is the author of *Baseball's Last Dynasty: Charlie Finley's Oakland A's* (which won the prestigious Seymour Award from the Society for American Baseball Research), *Roberto Clemente: The Great One,* and *The Orlando Cepeda Story.* For the Hall of Fame, he wrote numerous articles for publication, edited the Hall of Fame's Yearbook and quarterly newsletter, narrated Hall of Fame video productions, and interviewed most of the current living Hall inductees. Markusen is the regularly featured host of the "Hall of Fame Hour" on MLB Radio.

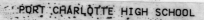